Editor: Thomas Keegan
Designer: Ben White
Illustrators: Kuo Kang Chen, Oxford
Illustrators, Liz Peperell, Cecilia
Fitzsimmons, David More

Kingfisher Books, Grisewood and Dempsey Ltd,
Elsley House, 24–30 Great Titchfield Street, London
W1P 7AD

First published in 1992 by Kingfisher Books.
The material in this edition was previously published in
Fun With Science: How Things Grow, Minibeasts, Trees and
Leaves, and Seasons in 1991.

© Grisewood and Dempsey Ltd 1991, 1992

British Library Cataloguing-in-Publication Data
A catalogue record for this book is available from the
British Library

ISBN 0 86272–852–5

Phototypeset by Wyvern Typesetting Ltd, Bristol
Printed and bound by the South China Printing Company,
Hong Kong

KINGFISHER

FUN WITH SCIENCE

NATURE

EXPERIMENTS • TRICKS • THINGS TO MAKE

ROSIE HARLOW & GARETH MORGAN

Kingfisher Books

Contents

BEFORE YOU START 8

How Things Grow

Introduction 10

SEEDS AND
GERMINATION 12
What Is a Seed? 14
Seeds on the Move 16

FLOWERS AND INSECTS 18
What Are Flowers For? 19
A Wild Flower Hunt 21
Flowers Without Petals 22
From Seed to Plant 24

PLANTS AND WATER 26
Green Deserts 28
Green Energy 30
Plants Store Food 32

THE GROWTH GAME 34
How Animals Grow 36
Food for Growth 40

Survival 42
Help a Bat 45

Humans Helping Out 46

HOW THINGS GROW
QUIZ 48

Minibeasts

Introduction 50

Looking for Minibeasts 52
Where Do Minibeasts Live? 54

METAMORPHOSIS 58
THE BUTTERFLY GAME 60
Moths and Butterflies 62

WATER MINIBEASTS 64
Make a Dragonfly 66
Predators and Prey 68

COLOUR AND
CAMOUFLAGE 71
Means of Protection 72
Make a Giant Ladybird 74

HELPFUL OR HARMFUL ? 76
Bees and Wasps 78
Ants 80

HOW WORMS HELP 82
Snail Watching 84

HELPING OUT 87

MINIBEAST QUIZ 88

Trees and Leaves

Introduction 90

WHAT IS A TREE?...................92
Tree Posters 94
Make a Tree 97

HOW DOES A TREE GROW?.....98
Twigs and Buds.................... 100

LEAVES 102
Why Trees Lose Their
Leaves................................. 106

WHERE DO TREES COME
FROM?................................ 110
Travelling Seeds.................... 112

THE TREE GAME 116
THE WORLD OF A TREE 118

WHO LIVES IN YOUR
TREE? 120
The Importance of Wood......... 122
Using Wood......................... 124
Disappearing Forests 126

TREES AND LEAVES
QUIZ 128

The Seasons

Introduction 130
What Season is it?.................. 132

WINTER............................... 134
Plants in Winter..................... 136
Animals in Winter.................. 138
Winter Activities 140

SPRING................................ 142
Plants in Spring 144
Animals in Spring 146
Spring Activities 148

SUMMER.............................. 150
Plants in Summer................... 152
Animals in Summer................ 152
Summer Activities.................. 156

AUTUMN 158
Plants in Autumn................... 160
Animals in Autumn................ 162
Autumn Activities.................. 164

SURVIVING THE SEASONS..... 166

SEASONS QUIZ 168

GLOSSARY........................... 169
INDEX 170

Before you start

This book is full of simple science experiments that will help you to discover more about how nature works. The four sections—How Things Grow, Minibeasts, Trees and Leaves, and The Seasons—are each divided into a number of topics. Where a new topic begins there is a blue line around the edge of the page.

You will be able to find most of the equipment you need for your experiments around the home. You do not need expensive equipment to make good biological investigations.

A word of warning

Some science experiments can be dangerous. Ask an adult to help you with difficult hammering or cutting and any experiments that involve flames, hot liquids or chemicals. Don't forget to put out any flames and turn off the heat when you have finished. Good scientists avoid accidents.

How to be a good scientist

- Collect all the equipment you need before you start.
- Keep a notebook. Write down what you see and hear.
- Make your observations very carefully. Sometimes things happen very quickly, and you may have to try a test more than once.

- If your test does not work properly the first time, try again or try doing it differently until you succeed.
- If your answers are not the same as those in the book, do not worry. It does not mean that you are wrong. See if you can work out what has happened and why.

Finding out more

- Make small changes in the design of the experiments and see if the results are still the same.
- Make up your own experiments and investigations to test your ideas about how animals and plants live.
- Do not worry if you do not understand all the things you see—there are always new things to discover.
- Remember that many of the most important discoveries were made by accident, and some of the greatest scientific theories are the simplest.

HOW THINGS GROW

This section of the book will help you to investigate how plants and animals grow.

There are eight main topics in this section:

- What a seed is and how it germinates
- How seeds move from place to place
- Flowers and insects
- How plants use water
- How plants use Sunlight
- How animals grow
- Surviving attacks by predators
- How humans can help

Use the symbols below to help you identify the three kinds of practical activities in this book.

EXPERIMENTS

TRICKS

THINGS TO MAKE

Introduction

All living things grow and reproduce. Green plants make seeds which grow into new plants. Animals produce eggs which grow into new animals. In this section you will find out the conditions that animals need in order to grow. You will discover the special conditions seeds require to germinate and you can discover why many plants make flowers before they make seeds.

Without plants there would be no animals. Plants provide the energy animals need to survive and grow. Plants also produce the oxygen that animals breathe. You can find out how the energy from the Sun gets passed along to all living things.

When conditions are good plants and animals grow quickly. When conditions are harsh growth is much slower. You can find how animals survive these conditions.

By doing the experiments and playing the games in this section you will be able to find the answers to the questions on these two pages.

WARNING!

Many plants are extremely poisonous and should not be eaten. Always check with an adult before you try any experiments which involve cooking or eating flowers, leaves, berries or fungi.

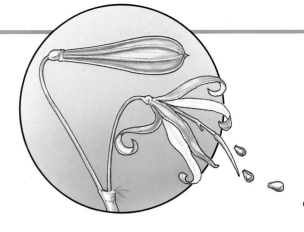

▲ How do seeds get around? (page 16)

▼ Do all plants make flowers? (page 23)

▼ What do plants need to grow? (page 24)

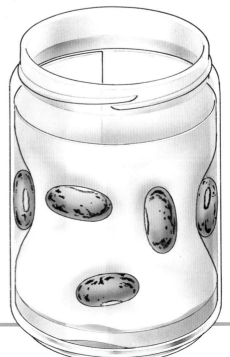

► How do animals grow? (page 37)

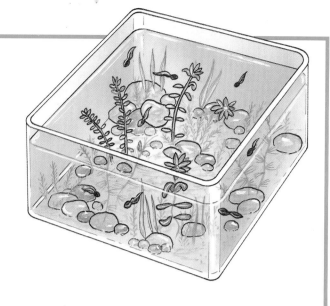

▼ Where do plants store energy? (page 32)

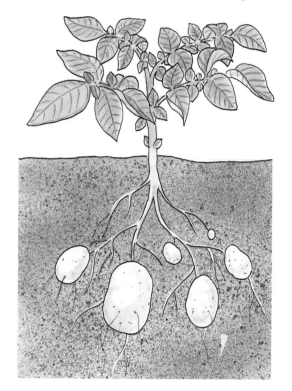

▲ Why is light so important? (page 30)

▼ How can you help animals to survive? (page 46)

▲ How do animals and plants survive in difficult conditions? (page 42)

Seeds and Germination

A huge oak tree starts life as an acorn two centimetres long. An apple tree grows from a little pip. All green plants start life as a small seed. These experiments will help you discover more about seeds and how they grow.

▲ Not all plants grow rooted to the ground. The plants here are living up a tree and getting all they need to grow from the air.

Experiments With Seeds

Seeds need certain conditions before they can start to grow, or **germinate**. These experiments will help you decide what these conditions might be.

Put cotton wool or tissue paper into each of the beakers and some seeds on top. Each of the beakers will be given different conditions which might help the seeds to germinate.

Beaker 1: Sprinkle with water each day and keep on a light windowsill.
Beaker 2: Keep on a windowsill – but add no water.
Beaker 3: Make sure the seeds are firmly held in the tissue paper. Fill the beaker up with water that has been boiled and left to cool.
Beaker 4: Sprinkle with water each day and keep in a fridge.
Beaker 5: Sprinkle with water each day and keep in a dark box in a warm place.

Look at the seeds each day for a week. Which factors help seeds to germinate – light, water, warmth, air?

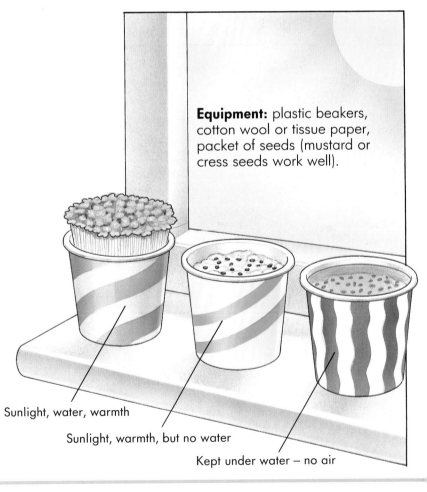

Equipment: plastic beakers, cotton wool or tissue paper, packet of seeds (mustard or cress seeds work well).

Sunlight, water, warmth

Sunlight, warmth, but no water

Kept under water – no air

Fun With Seeds

● Put some tissue paper into a saucer and dampen it. Arrange seeds on the paper in the shape of your initials. Keep the seeds damp and warm and watch the letters grow.

● Next time you eat a boiled egg keep the egg shell. Put some cotton wool inside, add some seeds and water them. The egg will start to grow 'hair', and you can draw a face on it. After a while you can cut the 'hair' and eat it!

Ancient Seeds

Seeds can lie dormant for hundreds of years before sprouting. It has even been claimed that seeds from Egyptian tombs have germinated after thousands of years.

Cress

Damp blotting paper

Egg shell

Water, kept in fridge

Water, warmth, dark

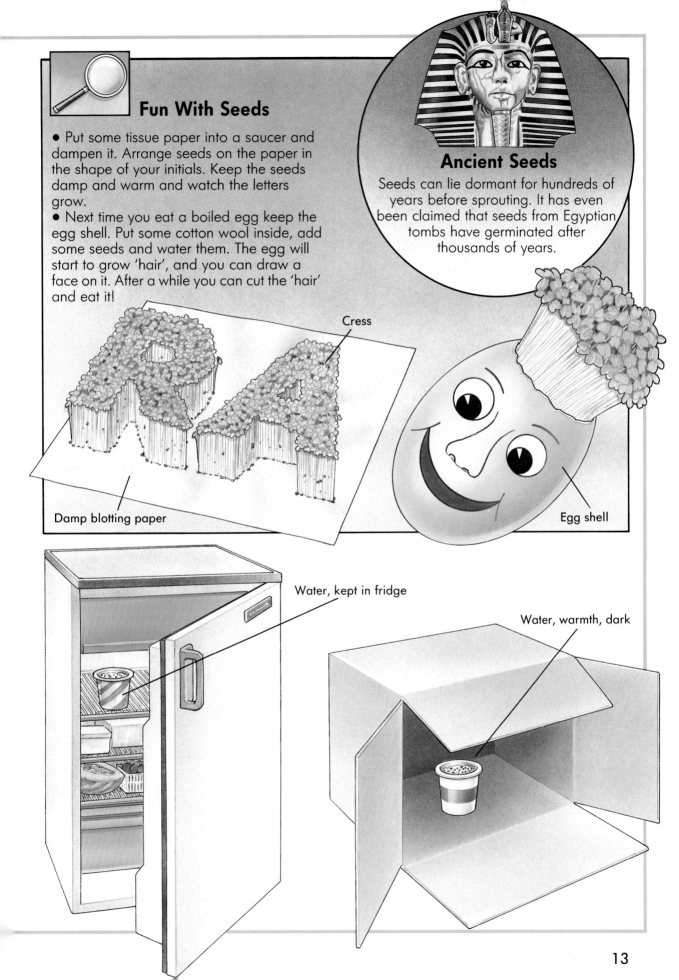

What is a Seed?

Seeds need air, water and warmth to germinate. For a seed to germinate, it needs these things in the right order. This section explores how germination is most likely to occur. You can also find out how to germinate some seeds that you can eat, and some that will grow into flowers.

Make Your Own Seeds

Tear the newspaper into strips. Paste the strips onto the balloon until the paper is about four pieces thick. Leave the balloon to dry overnight. When it is dry, cut a hole about 8 centimetres at one end. You can now paint the seed.

The Germination Game

You need six information tickets to go inside the seed. Write instructions on each ticket as follows:
1. Start to take in water
2. Start to take in oxygen
3. Use up stored food to start growing
4. Send out root
5. Send out shoot
6. Make new food in the leaves

Your seed is now ready to germinate. First you must throw a 1 with the dice. Take out ticket 1. Now the seed can start to take in water – it has started to germinate. You must now throw a 2 for the next ticket, then a 3. When you throw a 4 you can attach the root to the seed. Then a 5 means you can attach the shoot. Finally you must score the 6, and the seed will have germinated successfully.

   You must throw the numbers in the right order. All the stages in germination must happen in the right order. All the information needed to germinate is contained within a tiny seed, but it can only do so if the outside conditions are suitable.

Equipment: balloon, wallpaper paste, brush, card, paint or crayons, newspaper.

Make a leaf from paper. The plant needs leaves to make food.

The seed has a hard coat to keep out water and disease.

Information tickets

Make a yellow root. The plant needs a root to take in water and minerals.

Germinate Some Seeds

Equipment: plastic tray, potting compost, packets of vegetable seeds e.g. radish, cress, lettuce, mustard, flower seeds e.g. nasturtium, marigold.

You may be surprised how many seeds you can find in your kitchen. Some of these will germinate, although some have been treated so they can't. Put some blotting paper on a plate and spread some seeds on top. Make sure this is kept damp each day. If the seeds germinate they will be ready to eat after three days to a week. They can also be grown in a jar with muslin over the top. Try some of the following kitchen seeds and find out which germinate: lentils, rice, mung beans, chick peas, alfalfa.

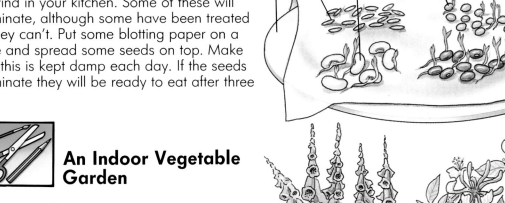

Rice   Beans   Chick peas   Mung beans

Plate

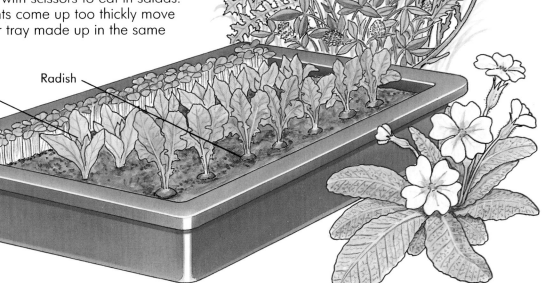

An Indoor Vegetable Garden

Equipment: plastic tray, potting compost, packets of vegetable seeds e.g. radish, cress, lettuce, mustard, flower seeds e.g. nasturtium, marigold.

Many of the vegetables we eat are grown from seed, and you can easily grow some of these yourself. Half fill a tray with potting compost and make it damp, but not soggy. Make lines across the compost with a stick and tip the seeds along the lines. Cover the seeds up again. Leave the tray somewhere warm and light and check each day that it is damp. Mustard and cress will grow quickly and can be cut with scissors to eat in salads. If the other plants come up too thickly move them to another tray made up in the same way.

Lettuce   Radish

Cress

Tray

Seeds On the Move

Next time you eat an apple, take the core apart and count how many seeds or pips there are inside. Imagine what would happen if all the apple pips in the windfall apples under an apple tree grew into new trees. Now try to calculate how many seeds a tree with 100 apples might make each year.

Not all seeds grow into new plants – try the calculation under the picture of the apple tree to find out what would happen if they all did. Many seeds land in a place where they cannot germinate, or are eaten by animals, and eventually they die. Even after germinating the plant is not safe – daisy plants growing in a lawn are regularly mown before they get a chance to grow fully.

It is important that a plant scatters its seeds over a wide area. This is called the **dispersal** of seeds. Some ways this is done are illustrated below. Certain seeds have little hooked hairs which stick onto animal fur or clothing. Many seeds are hidden within attractive fruits so that birds eat them.

Hooking onto animals

Spread by birds

Damp potting compost

Muddy shoe

Dispersed by plant

Spread by wind

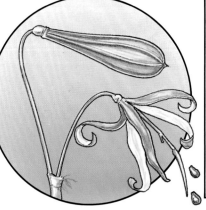

Automatic Collection

Next time you go for a walk, find out if you have been helping seeds to disperse. Scrape the mud from your shoes into a tray of potting compost and see if any plants grow. If they do you picked up seeds as you walked.

Flowers and Seeds

Plants **reproduce** (make more of themselves) by making lots of seeds. A few of these seeds germinate if the conditions are right, and grow into new plants. Apple pips, acorns, rice and mung beans are all seeds. This section examines how a plant makes a seed so that when it dies there are new plants to take its place.

▶ Look at this picture of a poppy. The seeds are forming in the pods at the centre of the flower.

Sunflowers can grow to 3.5 metres and have disk flowers, which come in many colours. Oil is extracted from their seeds.

Avocado stone

Cocktail stick

Water

Many other seeds can be used to grow plants at home. Try an avocado stone supported in a container of water. Pips and stones from all sorts of fruits can be grown.

The Seed Cycle

As a flower dies, the seeds start to form. These seeds can grow into new plants, which in turn make more flowers. When these die, more seeds are made again. This is known as a cycle and many events in nature occur in cycles. The seasons for example, and day and night. The seed cycle can take a very long time. If you plant an acorn it will be many years before the oak tree is old enough to make more acorns. However, you can watch the cycle happening much more quickly by using plant seeds. Sow some sunflower seeds indoors in damp potting compost during the spring. Remember to water them. When the weather becomes warm, plant the sunflower seedlings near a wall or fence which gets lots of sunshine. Put a tall stick in the ground to support the plant as it grows. Mark the stick each week to show how fast the plant is growing. Sunflowers can reach several metres in height. Once the plant has flowered the seeds form and you can collect these to grow some more plants the following year.

Flowers and Insects

Before a flower can make seeds it must be pollinated. Look at flowers outside on a warm day. You will usually find insects buzzing around them. It is very important that insects visit flowers because if pollination does not happen seeds will not form. Flowers try to make themselves attractive to insects in many ways.

Flowers and Colours

Bees can see certain colours well. Flowers have bright petals to encourage bees to visit. Many flowers have patterns on the inside of the petals which help the bee find the nectar. They are called honey guides and are often visible as strips of colour that lead into the centre of the flower where the nectar is stored. They are rather like runway landing lights which guide aeroplanes safely onto the ground. Some honey guides only show up in ultraviolet light.

Why Do Insects Visit Flowers?

Look at a bee or a butterfly as it visits a flower. Can you see its long **proboscis** (mouthpart)? The proboscis is stuck deep into the flower. You can discover what the insect is looking for by finding a flower of the white dead-nettle. Don't confuse it with a stinging nettle! Pull the flower from the plant, and gently squeeze along the tube towards the base of the flower. A small drop of nectar should appear. Taste the sweetness on your tongue. If there is no nectar, perhaps a bee has already taken it.

Flowers Smell Nice . . .

Flowers advertise themselves with smell as well as with colour. You can capture these lovely smells by making pot pourri. Ask if you can collect some petals from garden flowers. Rose petals are good for this. Dry them in a warm place like an airing cupboard, and put them in a small bowl.

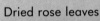

Dried rose leaves

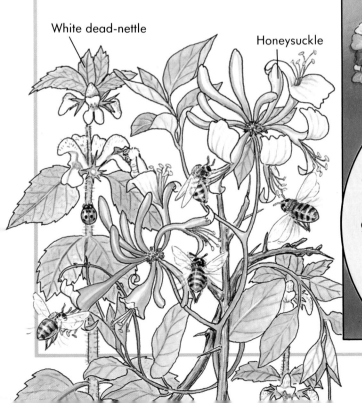

White dead-nettle

Honeysuckle

. . . and Nasty

Some flowers are pollinated by insects other than bees. Flies normally feed on dead and rotting material so flowers that need to attract flies for pollination make smells like bad meat. While the flies are investigating what they think is a tasty meal they pick up pollen and later transfer it to other flowers.

What Are Flowers For?

Flowers are the part of the plant that help to make sure that the plant reproduces and that the next generation of that plant is produced. Flowers contain the pollen and ova which together can make seeds which will grow into new plants.

Looking Inside a Flower

Every flower contains a range of very complicated structures, each with its own function to perform. The basic structures are shown below. To discover these for yourself, pick a common flower and cut it in half. You will then be able to see all the contents, such as the stamen, style, sepals and petals. If it is a flower that is fertilised by insects you will see the nectary at the base of the flower, where the insects seek out food.

A daisy is made up of many tiny flowers. They make a large landing platform for calling insects. These pick up pollen as they wander about the flower.

Foxgloves are pollinated by large bumble bees. The flower is shaped like a bell, the bee crawls inside to collect the nectar, and picks up pollen as it does so.

Yellow flowers such as the buttercup are a particular favourite of many small insects. Try wearing yellow clothes on a sunny day and see if insects visit you.

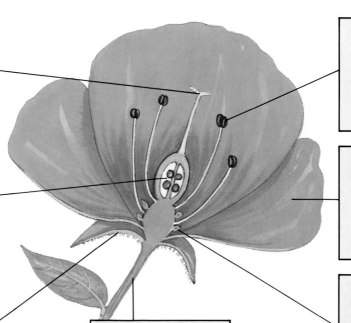

Stigma
This is the female part of the flower. When the pollen brushes off onto the stigma, pollination occurs.

Ovary
A pollen grain on the stigma grows down to the ovary. If it enters the ovary fertilisation occurs and a seed develops.

Sepals
These make a tough protective cover for the delicate flower to prevent damage when it is still in bud.

Stamen
The anthers contain pollen. Pollen sticks to insects when they visit, and is taken off to another flower.

Petals
The flower advertises itself to insects by having bright petals. Petals advertise that nectar is inside.

Nectaries
Where nectar is made. Without nectar insects would not visit, and pollination could not occur.

Stem
The stem needs to be strong enough to hold up the flower.

Make a Flower

Equipment: green and yellow coloured paper (or paper and paints), sticky tape, green bendy straw.

The best way to find out how a flower works is to make one yourself. You can even pollinate this model flower yourself.

Trace the shape of each part of the flower onto card. You will require five petals, five sepals, one stigma, six anthers, two leaves.

1. Poke the straw through the middle of the sepals.
2. Push the narrow end of the petals into the end of the straw. You may find it easier if you fold the narrow part of the petal down the middle first.
3. Push the stigma into the straw in the same way.
4. Arrange the anthers in a circle around the stigma by pushing them into the straw too.
5. Tape the leaves to the lower part of the stem.

   You can make different model flowers by changing the colour and number of petals. You can also vary the length and number of anthers and styles. There are many possible variations on the same basic idea. There are thousands of different flowers, and the next page will help you to identify some of them.

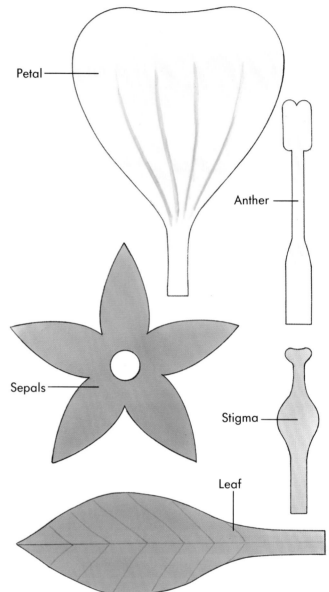

Petal

Anther

Sepals

Stigma

Leaf

Bendy straw

Pollinate Your Flower

Balance a small amount of baking flour on the anthers. Make your finger into a bee by painting it as shown. Put a small drop of honey right inside the flower to represent nectar. As it enters the flower, some of the 'pollen' will rub off onto its body.

'Finger bee'

A Wild Flower Hunt

Flowers come in many shapes and sizes. However, they need to attract insects to visit so pollination can occur. Many flowers have strange names because of the way they look, or because of stories that are told about them. People used to think that foxgloves were worn by foxes.

If you want to identify a flower, start off by making a flower chart. Draw a picture of the flower in the centre of a piece of paper, and fill out the information around the edge.

Number of flowers on stem
One

Shape of leaf

How many anthers?
Five

Is it alone or are there lots together?
Lots together

How many stigmas?
Two

How big is the flower?
Two cm across

Where is it?
In grass

How high is it off the ground?
Ten cm

How many petals does it have?
Four

What does it smell of?
Like apples

What colour is it?
Blue

What shape are the petals?

Pressing and Drying Flowers

The best method for pressing flowers is to place a clean sheet of paper in a large book and lay the flower on this. Cover it with a large piece of blotting paper and close the book. Pile other large books on top and your flower will be ready after a month. Some flowers can be dried without pressing, hang these up in a bunch somewhere warm.

Many wild flowers are protected by law. Use garden flowers unless you are sure a wild flower is very common.

Blotting paper

Pile of heavy books

Flowers Without Petals

Many flowers are fertilised by insects. Some flowers are fertilised in other ways so they don't need bright petals. There are likely to be seeds made from these flowers in your kitchen, and others close to your home.

A Grass Hunt

There are thousands of different sorts of grasses, and they are pollinated by the wind and not by insects. The seeds which develop are sometimes called grains. Next time you visit some rough grassland collect a variety of grass flowers and see if any match the shape of the ones shown. Although there are no petals or sepals, you may find feathery anthers and hairy stigmas.

Grind Your Own Flour

Grind the wheat underneath the pestle and remove the husks as they rise to the top.

Grasses In the Kitchen

Have a look in your kitchen for foods that come from grass, then group them together depending on which grass they come from. Flour comes from wheat, cornflakes from maize, and so on.

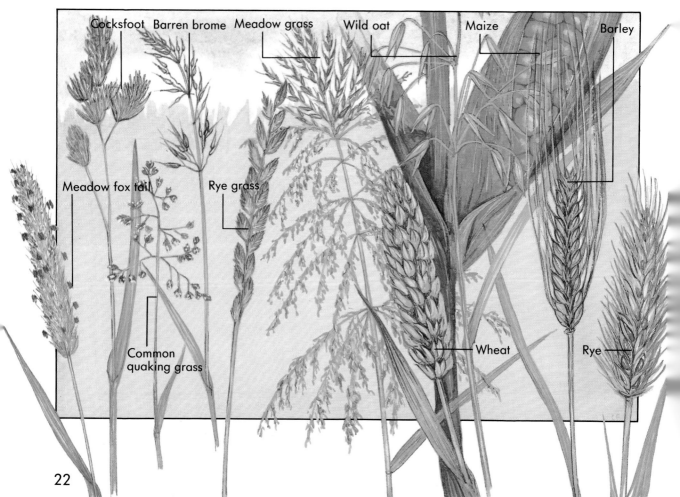

Cocksfoot · Barren brome · Meadow grass · Wild oat · Maize · Barley · Meadow fox tail · Rye grass · Common quaking grass · Wheat · Rye

Plants Without Flowers

You might think that many of these plants don't look much like plants at all. They don't have leaves and roots, and they never have flowers. This page tells you where to find them, and how to grow them.

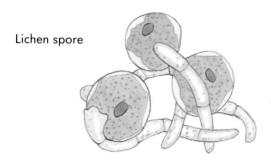

Lichen spore

▲ Gravestones are a good place to look for lichens. The bigger a lichen the older it is so look for them on the oldest headstones.

If the water in a pond is green it is usually because of millions of tiny green algae. Even magnified many times each one still looks like a tiny green blob. However, algae have an excellent way of making more algae. Each one in the water can split into two more, then each of the two algae formed can grow again. These can each divide into two new algae, and so on.

Lichens are fungi and algae growing together, and they reproduce by making spores. Look for lichens on trees, old walls and stones. They often look like flat pancakes and may be grey, green or orange. If you find many near you it means the air is clean. If there are few, the pollution in the air has killed many of them.

Algae under microscope

Jar

Tap water

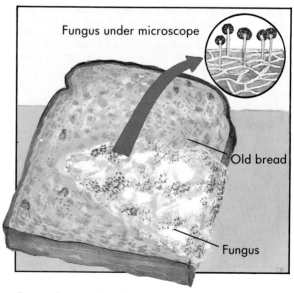

Fungus under microscope

Old bread

Fungus

Grow Some Algae

You can grow algae by placing a clear container of rain water on a sunny window-sill for a few days. The water will turn green as **spores** (seeds) of algae from the air quickly grow and divide.

Grow Some Fungi

Put an old piece of bread on some plastic and keep it damp for a few days. Look to see if grey or blue patches appear. These are fungi, developing from spores that have landed from the air.

From Seed to Plant

Seeds require certain conditions to germinate. In this section you can find out what conditions the plant needs to grow after it has germinated. Here are some suggestions of what a plant might require in order to grow: air, water, soil, gravity, light, fertiliser and darkness.

Does Gravity Affect Seeds, Roots and Shoots?

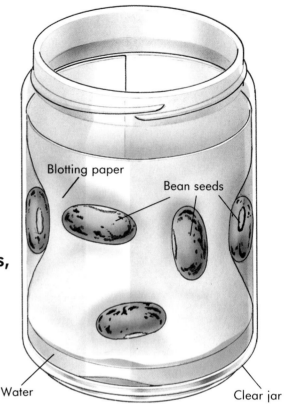

Blotting paper

Bean seeds

Water

Clear jar

The shoot of a plant will grow towards the light. However, seeds may be buried deep in the soil when they start to grow. This experiment examines whether a seed planted upside down grows downward with its roots in the air.

Tape the blotting paper into the jar as shown. Pour some water into the jar so that the blotting paper can soak it up. Place the beans between the paper and the jar in a variety of different positions; use a pencil to help. Place the jar in a completely dark cupboard and look at it each day. You will find that the roots still grow downwards and the shoot upwards. When there is no light the shoot responds to gravity. This is necessary because the seed is in darkness before the shoot emerges into the sunlight.

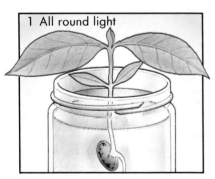

1 All round light

2 Kept in dark

3 Light from one side

4 Silver foil cap

Do Plants Need Light?

Equipment: four jars or plastic cups, broad bean seeds, cotton wool, silver foil.

Put cotton wool in each of the jars, and make it wet. Place two broad bean seeds in each cup. Check the seeds each day, and keep the cotton wool damp. Place the cups as follows:
1. In a place with light coming from all directions.
2. In a dark cupboard (or make a dark tube to cover it).
3. On a sunny windowsill.
4. As 3, but make a small foil cap to place over the shoot.

Does the Colour of Light Matter?

Equipment: small margarine or yoghurt tubs, tissue paper, sheets of coloured plastic or cellophane (e.g. clear, red, green), packet of cress seeds.

Put some damp paper in the bottom of each tub. Add some seeds, and place some coloured plastic over each tub. Place in a warm, light place. Check the tubs each day and water if necessary. Watch to see if the colour of light reaching the seedlings affects how they develop.

Clear plastic

Cress

Plastic tub

Coloured plastic

Green Plants Need Light

Seeds don't need light to germinate, and they can grow without light – at least for a while. But without light they can't turn green. This is because when there is no light they cannot make the green chemical **chlorophyll** in their leaves. Because it is so important for a plant to find the light, the tip of the shoot is able to detect where the light is coming from. The plant can then grow towards the light. Without chlorophyll the plant cannot make any vital sugars and growth cannot take place.

▶ Plants always grow towards the light. This is important to trees in a wood, otherwise they would get shaded out by their neighbours.

Plants and Water

Gravity causes the roots of a plant to grow downwards. The roots anchor the plant into the soil, and they also absorb water. This section looks at how much water a plant contains, how much it uses in a day and how the water is moved around the plant. You can find out what happens to this water.

Equipment: rice, cucumber, weighing scales, baking tray, baking paper.

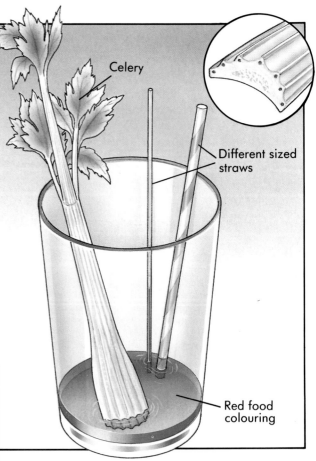

Water in Plants

Slice up some cucumber and weigh it on some baking paper. Measure the same weight of rice onto some more paper. Put them both on a baking tray along with some water in the jar top. Ask for the tray to go in the oven on a low heat. When the oven has

cooled look at the water in the jar top. If the tray has been in long enough the water will have evaporated. The same will have happened to the water inside the cucumber and the rice. Weigh them to see if they have lost water and got lighter.

How Does the Water Move Around?

Pour about 1 centimetre of water into the jar. Add a teaspoonful of red colouring and mix. Break off a piece of celery at the base and place it in the red water. Look at the celery each day to see where the red water goes. How long does it take to reach the leaf? After a few days cut the celery stalk into two and look for the red stain. It should be clear where you have cut across the tubes which carry the water up the stalk. The water rises by capilliary action. The smaller the tube, the higher the level. Put the straws in the glass, one thin, one wide. See in which the water rises further.

Equipment: glass of water, stick of celery, red food colouring, washing-up liquid, straws of varying widths (or an empty tube from an old biro).

Celery

Different sized straws

Red food colouring

Equipment: plastic bag, string, plant with big leaves.

Plastic bag

Rubber band or string

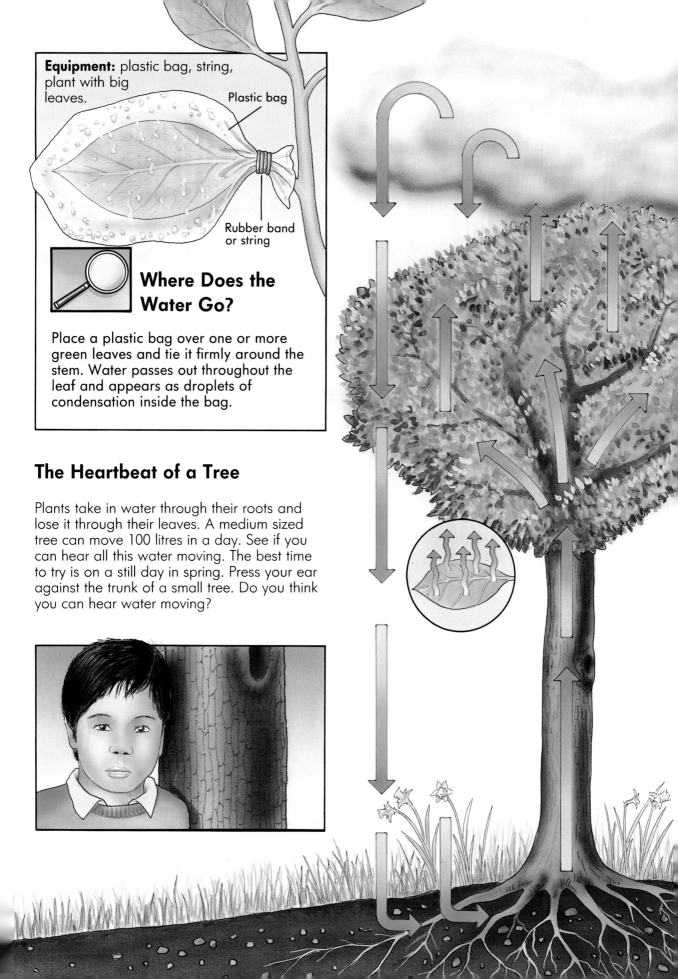

Where Does the Water Go?

Place a plastic bag over one or more green leaves and tie it firmly around the stem. Water passes out throughout the leaf and appears as droplets of condensation inside the bag.

The Heartbeat of a Tree

Plants take in water through their roots and lose it through their leaves. A medium sized tree can move 100 litres in a day. See if you can hear all this water moving. The best time to try is on a still day in spring. Press your ear against the trunk of a small tree. Do you think you can hear water moving?

Green Deserts

When a forest is chopped down the water cycle is broken. The rain is no longer taken up by the trees and there are no roots to hold the soil. Often the soil is washed away and the area turns into a desert. Because there are no trees, transpiration does not occur, and clouds can't form in the dry air. In many parts of the world deserts are getting bigger as more and more trees are cut down. The water cycle can be started up again, however. Tough trees can be planted in the deserts to hold the soil and start cycling the water again.

▶ Desert plants have to survive on very little water. They have very long roots to tap deep water sources, which helps to move water from the soil into the atmosphere.

Leaves Give Off Something Else

Equipment: small tub of water, funnel, another tub to go over the funnel, Canadian pondweed.

Arrange the equipment as shown. The jar upside-down over the funnel must be full of water. You may find this easier by setting up the experiment under water in a sink. Start the experiment in bright light, and watch to see if bubbles start forming. Move the experiment to a shady place and see if the bubbles appear more or less quickly. The bubbles coming off consist of a most important gas. This gas is **oxygen** and it is given off by all green leaves. Oxygen is one of the gases in the air all around you, and it is the one your body absorbs when you breathe in. All animals need oxygen to stay alive. This is another reason why plants are so important. If there were no plants there would be no oxygen to breathe.

If a glowing splint relights in a jar of gas – the gas is oxygen. Ask an adult to try this for you.

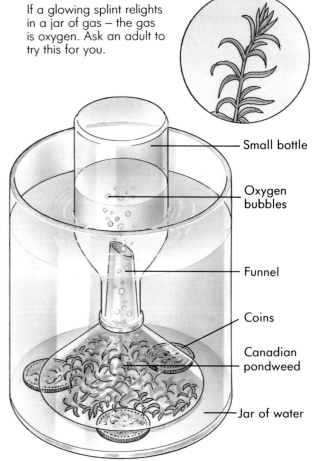

Small bottle

Oxygen bubbles

Funnel

Coins

Canadian pondweed

Jar of water

A Bottle Garden

Equipment: large plastic sweet jar with lid, gravel, soil, small plants (see below).

The water transpiring from a leaf becomes visible when a bag is put over it. This **condensed** water can be used again by the plant if it is absorbed through the roots. This bottle garden uses water in this way. Put some gravel or small stones in the jar and lay it on its side. Add a layer of damp soil or compost. Choose some small plants from your garden or a nursery. Some ideas are illustrated but ask for advice. Press the plants into the soil with a long stick, and attach the lid tightly. Put the jar in a light place, but not in direct sunlight. The plants in the bottle use the water in the soil and the carbon dioxide in the air to make sugar. They give off oxygen as they do this. At night when there is no light to help photosynthesis the plants use the energy in their food stores, they respire.

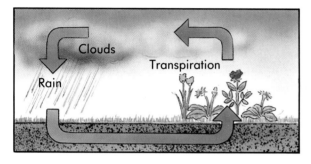

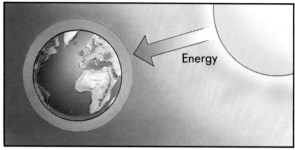

A cycle in the bottle

Our Earth relies on a water cycle. The plants transpire water which condenses as clouds. The water falls back as rain which the plants can use again.

Bottle garden maintenance

Make sure that you keep the bottle garden clean. Place it where it is in sunlight and somewhere reasonably cool. Make sure the lid fits tightly.

A cycle in the Earth

The total amount of water on Earth is nearly constant. No water arrives or leaves. There is only one thing which reaches the Earth from outside and that is sunlight.

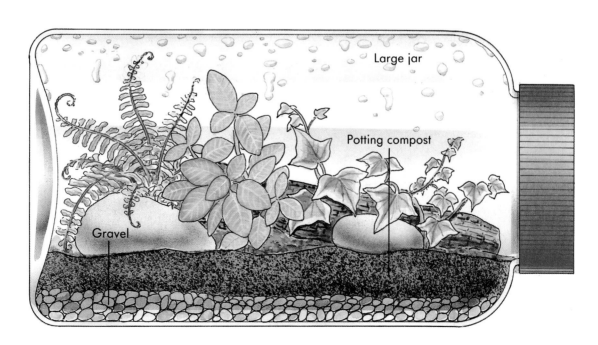

Green Energy

The last section showed that plants need water and sunlight, and that they give off oxygen. In this section you can find out what they use the sunlight for, and what happens if plants are kept in the dark. You will find out that oxygen is not the only thing that plants make which we need.

Plants In the Dark

For this experiment you will need a brick with a frog (dip) in one side. Place the brick with the frog face down on an area of green grass (but ask an adult first as this will spoil the lawn!). Each day carefully look under the brick and then replace it in exactly the same place. Compare the grass underneath the brick with the rest of the lawn. The grass will go yellow because it was hidden from the light.

Brick

Grass

Food Producers

Animals obtain their energy to live and grow by eating. Green plants have to make their own food. They do this in their leaves. The green chemical in the leaves is called **chlorophyll**. It is the chlorophyll which converts sunlight energy into food energy. It does this by combining water (taken in by the roots) and carbon dioxide gas (taken in through the leaves) to form sugars. When there is no light, sugars cannot be made, and eventually the plant will die.

As the sugars are produced, oxygen is formed as a waste product and is given out by the leaf along with surplus water. So plants are vital to us in two ways. They give out oxygen for us to breathe, and they make food energy which we can eat.

Which Plants Like the Light?

Equipment: hoop, or square 50–100 centimetres across, pencil and paper.

Throw the hoop a short way over your shoulder. Record how many different sorts of plant there are inside your hoop, and identify any if you can. Try and record if there are different types of grass or only one. You will find that some plants prefer the shade, some prefer light areas.

Did You Know?

Some plants do not make their own food, or make only a limited amount. They are called parasitic plants. They attach suckers to the stems or roots of another plant and steal the food that it makes. Some other plants supplement their food by eating insects. Different species use hinged leaves, sticky hairs or long, waxed funnels to catch their prey. The insect is slowly dissolved in the plant's digestive fluids.

Plants Store Food

The food a plant makes is transported around the plant to where it is needed. However, the plant may not need energy straight away, so the food must be stored. This reserve of food may be used later for a variety of reasons: to help the plant survive the winter, to assist in the formation of seeds and fruits. Animals and people can eat much of the food that plants store.

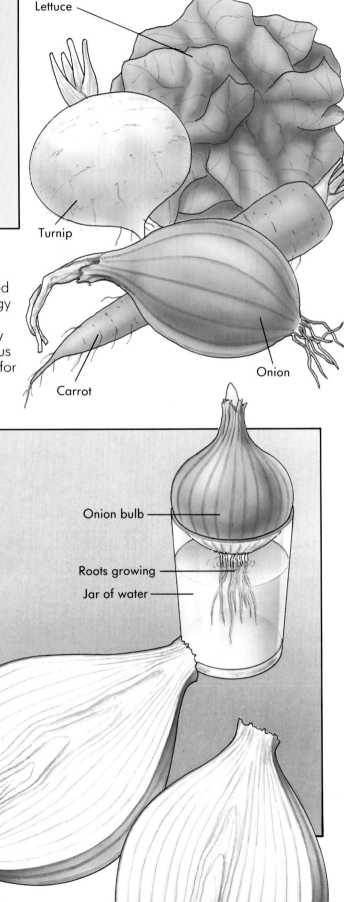

Lettuce

Turnip

Carrot

Onion

Vegetable Food Sources

The sugars made in the leaves can be stored as sugar, or converted into other high energy substances like fats or carbohydrates. Eat some lettuce leaves and try to decide if they contain much sugar or carbohydrate. Various parts of a plant can be used to store food, for example the root or the stem.

Cut Up an Onion

Each of the 'shells' in an onion is a swollen leaf. You can show that these shells are leaves by letting an old onion grow. Rest it on a jar full of water and watch it develop. Roots will grow from the hard bottom part – this is the tiny stem – and the top of the swollen leaves will start to shoot. At the same time the onion 'shells' will start to shrivel as the food in them is used up.

Onion bulb

Roots growing

Jar of water

Onion cut in two

Swollen base of leaf

Why Do Plants Store Food?

Plants store food in roots (carrots), stems (potatoes) and leaves (onions). What is this food used for? The experiment with the onion shows that the stored food can be used to start the plant growing again. This is useful after the winter because all the growing parts of the plant have died back. When the warm weather starts the plant can grow up again quickly using the stored food energy. So a plant with stored food has an advantage over a plant growing from seed.

Grow a Carrot Top

Use a carrot top that still has leaves. Put it in water, and look for new roots forming.

▲ The exact food stored varies from plant to plant. Potatoes store food as starch. Much of the sugar we eat comes from sugar cane.

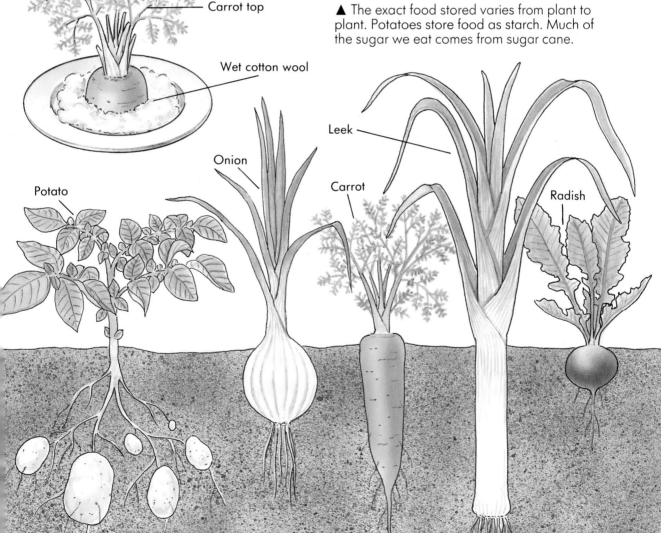

Carrot top

Wet cotton wool

Potato

Onion

Leek

Carrot

Radish

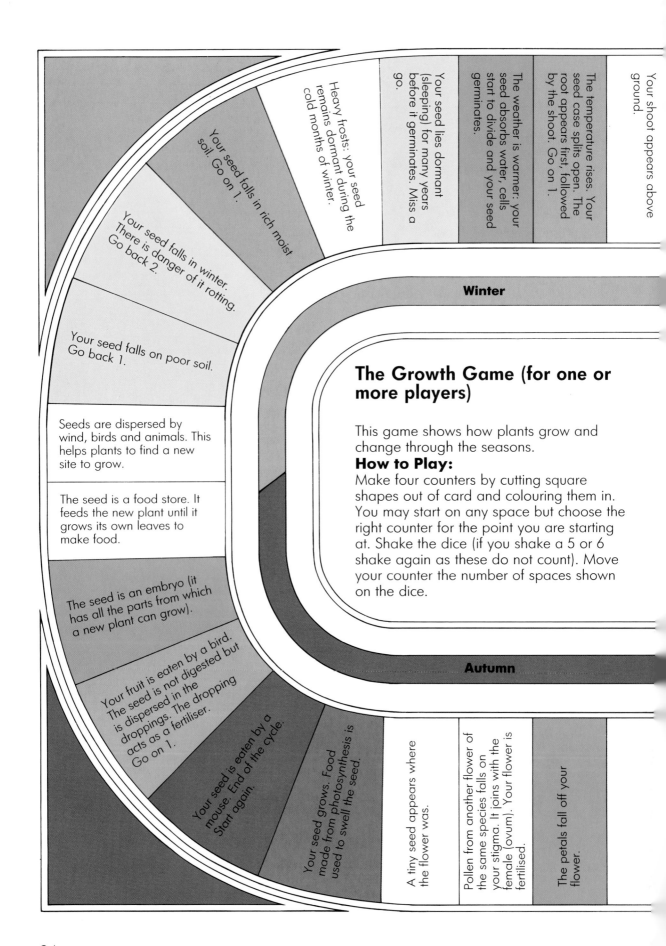

Your shoot appears above ground.

The temperature rises. Your seed case splits open. The root appears first, followed by the shoot. Go on 1.

The weather is warmer; your seed absorbs water, cells start to divide and your seed germinates.

Your seed lies dormant (sleeping) for many years before it germinates. Miss a go.

Heavy frosts: your seed remains dormant during the cold months of winter.

Your seed falls in rich moist soil. Go on 1.

Your seed falls in winter. There is danger of it rotting. Go back 2.

Your seed falls on poor soil. Go back 1.

Seeds are dispersed by wind, birds and animals. This helps plants to find a new site to grow.

The seed is a food store. It feeds the new plant until it grows its own leaves to make food.

The seed is an embryo (it has all the parts from which a new plant can grow).

Your fruit is eaten by a bird. The seed is not digested but is dispersed in the droppings. The dropping acts as a fertiliser. Go on 1.

Your seed is eaten by a mouse. End of the cycle. Start again.

Your seed grows. Food made from photosynthesis is used to swell the seed.

A tiny seed appears where the flower was.

Pollen from another flower of the same species falls on your stigma. It joins with the female (ovum). Your flower is fertilised.

The petals fall off your flower.

Winter

Autumn

The Growth Game (for one or more players)

This game shows how plants grow and change through the seasons.

How to Play:

Make four counters by cutting square shapes out of card and colouring them in. You may start on any space but choose the right counter for the point you are starting at. Shake the dice (if you shake a 5 or 6 shake again as these do not count). Move your counter the number of spaces shown on the dice.

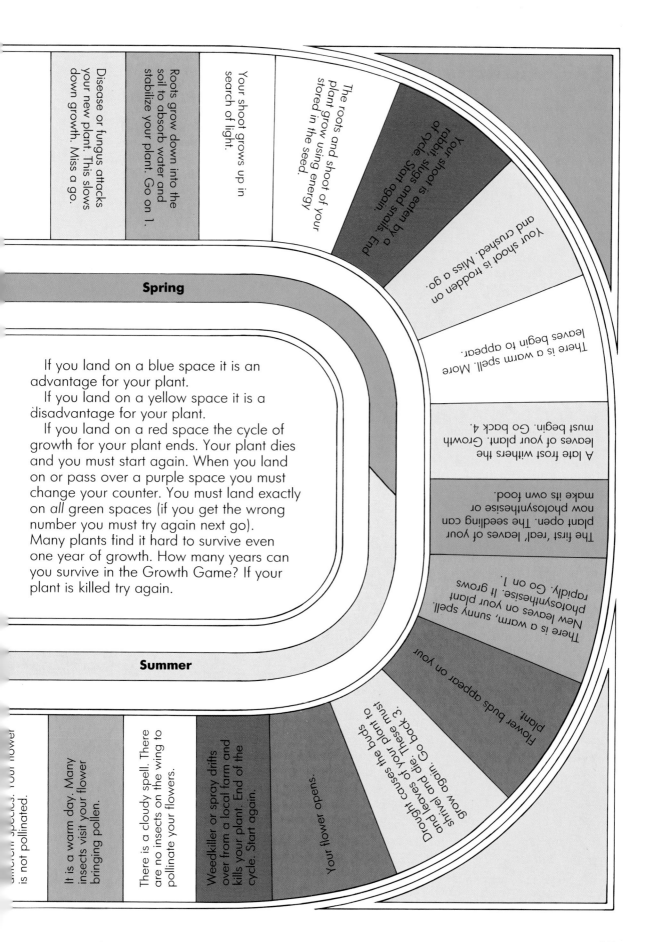

If you land on a blue space it is an advantage for your plant.

If you land on a yellow space it is a disadvantage for your plant.

If you land on a red space the cycle of growth for your plant ends. Your plant dies and you must start again. When you land on or pass over a purple space you must change your counter. You must land exactly on *all* green spaces (if you get the wrong number you must try again next go). Many plants find it hard to survive even one year of growth. How many years can you survive in the Growth Game? If your plant is killed try again.

Spring

Disease or fungus attacks your new plant. This slows down growth. Miss a go.

Roots grow down into the soil to absorb water and stabilize your plant. Go on 1.

Your shoot grows up in search of light.

The roots and shoot of your plant grow using energy stored in the seed.

Your shoot is eaten by a rabbit, slug and snails. End of cycle. Start again.

Your shoot is trodden on and crushed. Miss a go.

There is a warm spell. More leaves begin to appear.

A late frost withers the leaves of your plant. Growth must begin. Go back 4.

The first 'real' leaves of your plant open. The seedling can now photosynthesise or make its own food.

There is a warm, sunny spell. New leaves on your plant photosynthesise. It grows rapidly. Go on 1.

Flower buds appear on your plant.

Drought causes the buds and leaves of your plant to shrivel and die. These must grow again. Go back 3.

Summer

Your flower opens.

Weedkiller or spray drifts over from a local farm and kills your plant. End of the cycle. Start again.

There is a cloudy spell. There are no insects on the wing to pollinate your flowers.

It is a warm day. Many insects visit your flower bringing pollen.

different species. Your flower is not pollinated.

35

How Animals Grow

Different creatures grow at different rates. A rabbit becomes adult when it is only four months old. A greenfly can grow up in three days. Human beings may still be growing after 15 years. Young animals sometimes look like a small version of the adult (for example a human baby) and sometimes completely different (for example a caterpillar, which turns into a butterfly).

Look At an Egg

In one sense all animals start life as an egg. In some cases the young animal has developed from the egg before the mother gives birth. Mammals, including humans, are an example of this. With other animals, the egg has a protective covering and is laid by the mother. The young animal develops inside the egg and then hatches out. Crack open a chicken's egg into a saucer and see if you can find the parts marked on the left-hand diagram.

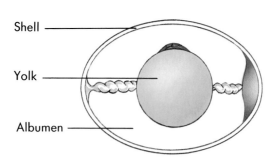

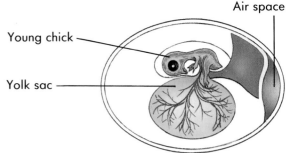

Look for the 'blood spot'. This is the part that could develop into a chick. However, most chicken eggs have not been fertilised by the male so this cannot happen. When you boil an egg, prick it at the blunt end. It is when the air in this expands that the egg cracks.

How Snails Grow

Water snails lay eggs that are easy to see. Look for lines of jelly underneath leaves in water where they live. The tiny dots inside are the eggs. Look at them every day with a hand lens and watch the snails take shape. The eggs of garden snails are hard to find in the wild, but easy if you keep snails at home. As young snails grow the shells become stronger. When they are strong enough you can mark the edge of a shell with ink each week to see how fast it grows.

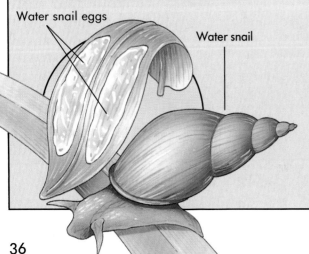

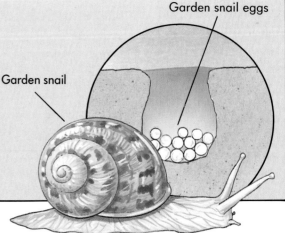

How Frogs Grow

Collect a small amount of frog spawn from a pond. Make sure you have permission to do this. Keep the spawn in a large plastic tank, using water taken from the pond. Cover the tank to stop the water evaporating. Keep the tank somewhere cool, but not too cold, and out of the sun. After the tadpoles have hatched, choose a few to keep and return the rest to the pond. Tadpoles will eat algae in the tank, but as they grow they need extra nutrients. When they are big enough hang a piece of raw meat in the tank for them to eat.

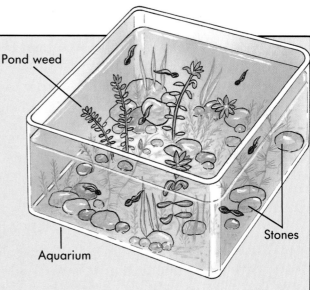

Pond weed

Stones

Aquarium

Spawn   **Tadpole**   **12 weeks**   **Froglet**

Gills

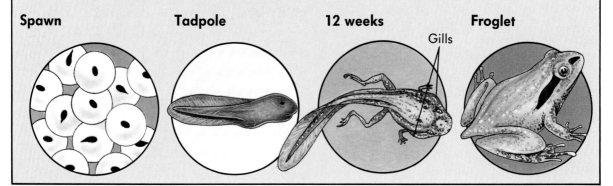

How Reptiles Grow

As a tadpole grows it changes shape entirely. This is called **metamorphosis**. You may be able to think of what sort of metamorphosis a butterfly shows as it grows from an egg. Reptiles grow in an equally surprising way. Snakes and lizards do not change shape as they grow, but shed their skins, which will only stretch so much before they have to be replaced. Each time they do this there is a new skin underneath. Many reptiles are rare, and some dangerous, so it is not a good idea to keep them as pets.

Old skin

Watching Woodlice

Woodlice belong to the same group of animals as crabs – the **crustaceans**. They are quite easy to keep, but remember that crustaceans lose water easily and so must be kept in damp surroundings. Use a plastic tub with soil in the bottom; add some bark and leaves. Put in a container of water to keep the air damp. Put the woodlouse box somewhere cool and shady. Stock it with woodlice found under logs and stones. Like reptiles, woodlice shed their skins. Look under their bodies for eggs or young.

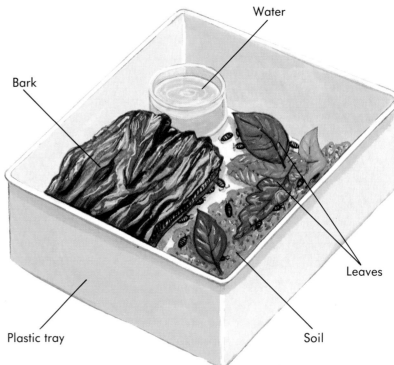

Water

Bark

Leaves

Soil

Plastic tray

Keeping Stick Insects

It is possible to get hold of stick insects from pet shops, wild life parks with insect houses and sometimes schools. Remember to ask what plants they feed on and how to look after them. Make sure you have plenty of food near your house (usually privet leaves or bramble). A large plastic sweet jar with holes in the lid makes a good container. Be careful to clean them out and provide fresh food for them.

They are fascinating creatures to keep. Watch the way they grow by shedding their skin. Try to get a male and female so they can mate and produce young. Look out for eggs. They can take up to a month to hatch so be patient.

Plastic jar

Lid

Privet leaves

Mammals

You belong to a group of animals known as mammals. Other mammals include elephants, dogs, lions, and bats. Mammals have certain things in common. They are born alive, not as an egg. They drink milk from their mother. They have hair covering part of their body. Their blood stays at a constant warm temperature. Most other creatures, except birds, have a body temperature that changes as the temperature of the environment changes. Different mammals grow at different rates. This chart compares how a rabbit and a deer grow. You could try drawing up a similar chart for other mammals, like your pet, or even yourself.

Growing Up

The chart below shows how long four different animals take to reach adulthood. Young humans take about 12–15 years to reach maturity. All the animals below are smaller and take much less time.

▲ Two types of young mammal *above* a young deer and *below* baby rabbits. Both are able to move very soon after birth to avoid predators.

	Mole	Deer	Squirrel	Rabbit
How long is the young animal inside the mother?	1 month	8 months	1–2 months	1 month
How many babies are born at a time	about 4	1 (sometimes 2)	3–6	About 6
How many litters can be born in a year?	usually 1	1	1 or 2	Up to 7
How many young are born in a year?	about 4	Usually 1	up to 12	10 to 20
How long does the mother suckle (give milk to) the young?	1 month	Up to a year	up to 2 months	1 month
Can the new-born mammal see?	no	yes	no	no
Can the new-born mammal walk?	no	yes	no	no
Does it have a good layer of fur?	no	yes	no	no
When is it ready to leave the mother?	1 month	1 year	3 months	1 month
When is it ready to have its own young?	1 year	2 or 3 years	6 months	4 months

Food for Growth

Most plants make their own food, using carbon dioxide and water. This is called photosynthesis. Animals cannot make their own food so they have to eat to get their energy. Some animals eat plants; these are known as **herbivores**. Some animals eat other animals and these are called **carnivores**. If an animal eats both plants and animals it is an **omnivore**.

A Food Chain

A plant (the wheat) captures the energy of the Sun by photosynthesis. This energy is stored in the wheat grains. When a herbivore (the mouse) eats the plant, the stored food energy can now be used by the herbivore. When a carnivore (the owl) eats the herbivore, the food energy is passed on again. Work out some food chains that you are part of. You should find that everything you eat depends at some point on the energy from the Sun.

A Food Chain Mobile

Copy the shapes of an owl, a mouse and a piece of grain onto card, and then cut around the thick black lines. You should then have five separate pieces: a hollow owl, a hollow mouse, a piece of wheat and two eyes. To build the mobile, thread the pieces using a needle and thread as follows. Thread the wheat at W and hang it from the mouse at A. Thread the mouse at X and hang it from the owl at B. Thread the owl's eyes at Y (hang from C) and at Z (hang from D). Finally thread the owl at V so it can be hung up. Colour in the mobile before hanging it up.

Equipment: card, scissors, thread, needle, paint or crayons.

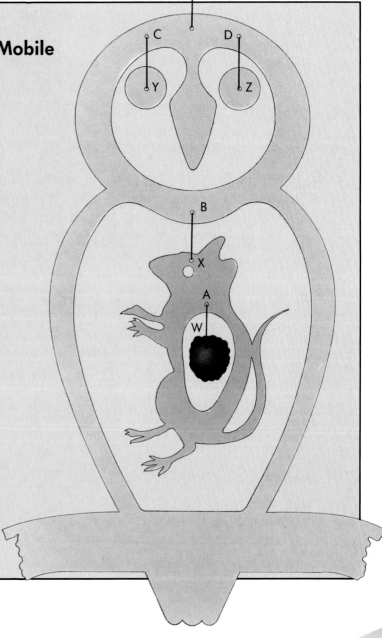

A Food Web

An owl does not only eat mice. It might also eat worms or small birds. A mouse might eat fruit as well as wheat. Small birds might eat worms, or fruit, or caterpillars. Draw and cut out pictures of various plants and animals. Try to link them into food chains. You will soon find that the foods are joined in a complicated web like the one below. Play this food web game. Make 20 yellow counters out of card. Place these on the Sun to represent the energy that comes from the Sun.

 ## Play the Game

On your own, or taking turns with someone else, move one counter at a time to one of the plants. You can now move any counter at any time – from Sun to plant, from plant to animal, or from animal to animal. Counters can only be moved away from the Sun, to show the movement of energy as food is eaten. If two or more counters reach one space, pile them up and then move them together. Keep moving counters until you have no more arrows to follow.

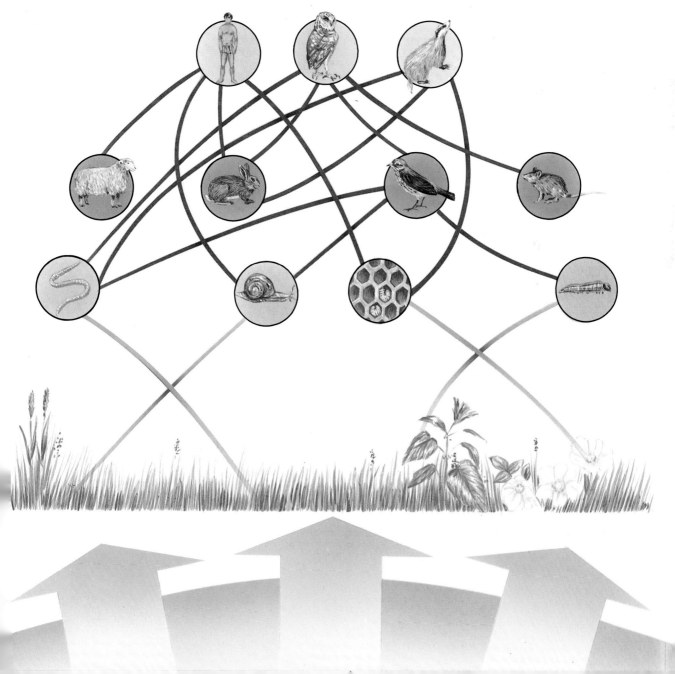

Survival

All living things need water. Green plants need sunlight to make food, while animals eat to get their energy. Some animals eat decaying matter, and are called **scavengers**. Vultures are scavengers. Sometimes food and light are hard to come by, so some plants and animals need to change their lifestyles in order to survive.

Surviving Drought

The driest places in the world are the deserts, for example the great Sahara. Very icy places are deserts too: there is plenty of water, but it is all locked up as ice. To survive drought, plants and animals need to be able to use quickly any rain that does fall. The spadefoot toad can exist without water in its burrow for months, but will emerge quickly if rain falls. A cactus in the desert will wait years for a rainshower, then suddenly it will flower.

Spadefoot toad

Bactrian camel

Cactus

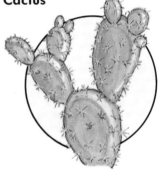

Eating to the Limit

Shrews have a constantly high demand for energy. Each day a shrew must eat its own weight in food – up to 10 grams. Imagine what this means. Weigh yourself, and then weigh out a kilogram of potatoes. Now calculate how many potatoes you would need to eat if you had to eat your own weight in food. The task is most difficult for shrews in the winter because there is a shortage of food and many die.

How many potatoes would you have to eat every day to consume your own weight?

Keeping Warm

Equipment: four identical jars with lids, hot water, themometer.

The experiment must be done on a cold day. Pour an equal amount of hot water from a jug into each of the four jars. Use the thermometer to check that the water is the same temperature in each jar. Now look around outside for good places to put one pot where it will hold its warmth. Put one of the pots out in the open and wrap another in

Both dormice (*above*) and bats (*below*) hibernate in the winter. Their body temperature can fall as low as 0°C.

The jar in the open will lose heat very quickly, like our unprotected skin would in cold places.

The jar with leaves around it will keep quite warm, though they do not insulate all that well.

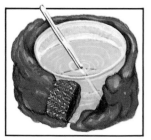

This jar will stay the warmest. The dry cloth provides good insulation much like an animal's coat.

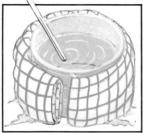

A wet cloth will cool the water quickly. The evaporating water in the cloth draws heat from the water in the jar.

leaves. Put a wet cloth around one, and a dry one around another. After ten minutes, use the thermometer (or your little finger) to see which jars have kept their heat and which have gone cold. Keep checking the water at intervals to see which one stays hot the longest. Do you think you would have survived the winter?

How to Survive the Cold

The only way a shrew can survive cold winters is to keep eating to provide energy. Mammals and birds differ from other animals because much of their energy is used to keep themselves warm. One way some mammals save energy in the winter is to let their body become much cooler. This is rather like keeping the temperature in your house at 10°C instead of 20°C in the winter. A lot less fuel would be needed.

Outwitting the Winter

This game is best played with two or more people. One person becomes a swallow with a thin pointed beak (the paper clip). The other is a thrush with a thicker beak (the peg). The foods on offer are seeds (the nuts) and soft creatures (the raisins). Use your 'beak' to start 'feeding', and store the food in front of you. In the summer both birds find insects best to eat. In autumn these run out, so the swallow **migrates**.

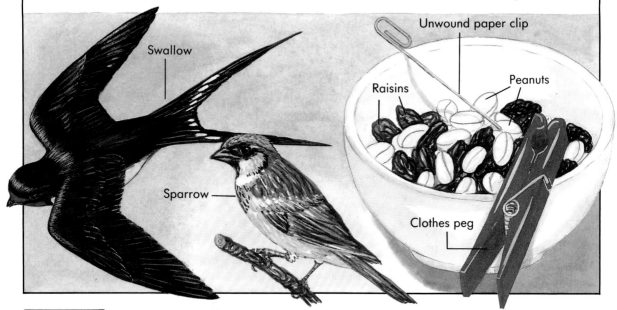

Swallow

Sparrow

Unwound paper clip

Raisins

Peanuts

Clothes peg

Sun Seekers

The body temperature of many creatures changes to match the temperature of the surroundings. Snakes and lizards sun themselves to increase their body temperature. Try this experiment in the summer to see if this is true for other creatures. Mark out 10 metres along a flower border. Walk slowly along this trail on a sunny day, noting how many insects there are. Do the same on a cool, cloudy day. Which creatures come out on the shady day?

Build a Bat Nesting Box

Equipment: You will need an adult to help with this. A plank of untreated wood one metre long, 20 centimetres wide, 2.5 centimetres thick, saw, nails, hammer.

The wood must never have been treated because the chemicals used might poison the bats. If it isn't rough, make grooves in it with the saw. Mark the plank as shown, and cut out the pieces. Nail the back through to the side pieces. Nail the top to the sides. Nail the front to the sides, bevelling the top edge if possible to make a good fit. Nail in the bottom piece, leaving the gap against the back: this is where the bats will get in and out. Tack on some old rubber to seal between the back and lid. It is best to make three boxes and then space them around a tree trunk about 3 or 4 metres off the ground. The boxes can be nailed on but be careful as this can damage the tree.

You should not try to look in the box. Bats are very easily scared, and in some countries it is illegal to disturb them. Watch the box at dusk to see if any emerge, and look for tiny black droppings under the box. You may even be able to hear the high pitched squeak that the bats make as part of their echo location.

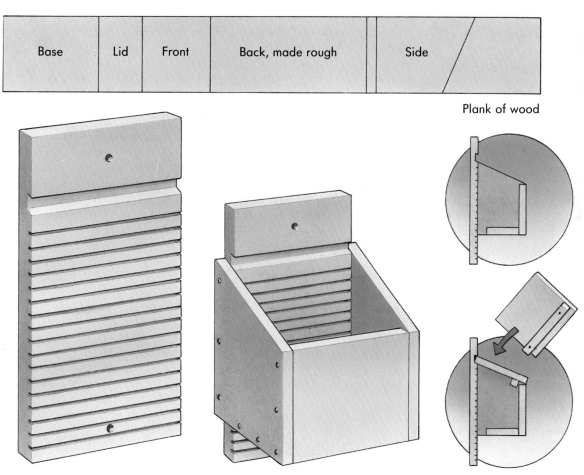

Plank of wood

The grooves in the back of the box are for the bats to hang on to. When they rest bats hang upside-down and need foot-holds, like those they would use in the wild.

Using nails to support the box can damage small trees. Another way of doing it is to use a length of old tyre inner tube stretched through the box and around the tree.

Be very careful of disturbing the bats if they nest in your box. In many countries they are protected by law and disturbing nesting bats can be an offence.

Humans Helping Out

For some animals staying alive, especially during the winter, can be a great problem. It is quite normal for many animals to die at this time of year. Many animals face extra problems because of the way humans behave.

Make a Bird Table

Use a piece of outdoor plywood, about 50 × 30 centimetres, up to 1 centimetre thick. Screw on thin wood strips from underneath to stop the seed blowing off, but leave gaps in the corners for drainage and cleaning. Attach the table to a post dug into the ground. Add some nails or hooks for hanging out nuts and bones. Paint with a non-toxic preservative and let it dry completely.

Clean it often with a stiff brush. If bird droppings build up around the base move the table occasionally.

Making Bird Pudding

This recipe for bird pudding is a good way of using up many kitchen scraps. Ask for a bowl of hot but not boiling water. Put a smaller bowl into the water and add the suet. Let it melt then stir in the scraps. Before the mixture hardens pour it into a yoghurt pot or half a coconut shell. This should have had a hole made in the bottom and string threaded through. It can be hung up to attract the acrobatic birds, but for other birds you should put some of the mixture on a bird table.

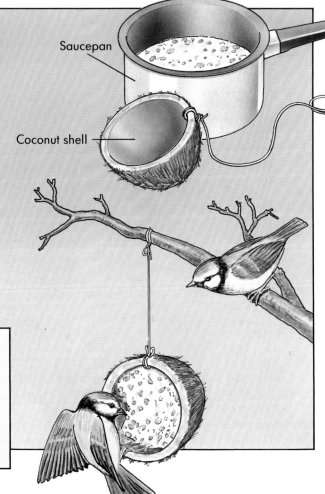

Saucepan

Coconut shell

Equipment: hot water in a bowl, equal amounts of suet and food or food scraps. The following may be used: bread, seeds, dried fruit, apples, bacon, oats. Do not use desiccated coconut or very salty foods.

Make a Nut Holder

Equipment: plastic bottle, string, scissors, peanuts.

Ask an adult to make two holes in the bottom of the bottle, on opposite sides. Thread string through these so the bottle can be hung upside down. Draw a line around the bottle about half way up. Ask for about ten holes to be made along this. Use these to cut slits down the bottle. Funnel the peanuts in through the top and replace the lid. Hang the bottle up. If the birds can't get a grip, push a stick right through two opposite slits.

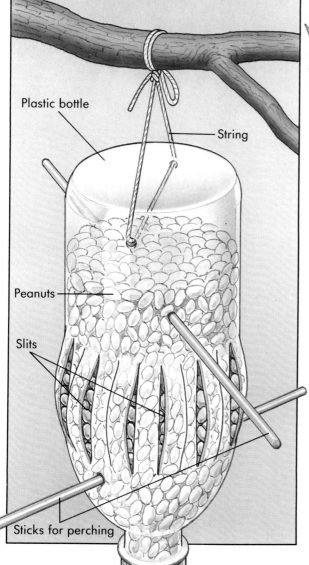

Plastic bottle

String

Peanuts

Slits

Sticks for perching

Helping With Housing

Often gardens and parks are too tidy for insects to find food and make a home. You can help by asking to have a small wild corner by a fence or hedge. Put down logs and flat stones. Let the grass grow up, and make sure the area isn't sprayed. The minibeasts that make a home here will in turn provide food for larger animals.

Bathtime

Bird baths are useful all through the year. An old dustbin lid is fine, or a tray, but the inside must be rough and not slippery. Put a few stones in and make sure to change the water daily. If it freezes melt it with warm water. Birds will drink in it, and also bathe to keep their feathers in good shape.

How Things Grow Quiz

1. A carnivore likes to eat plants.

2. Animals can make their own food using sunlight energy.

3. Green leaves make oxygen.

4. Plants convert sunlight energy to food energy by photosynthesis.

Answers

3. *True. Leaves give off oxygen when they photosynthesize.*

2. *False. Animals cannot make their own food and have to eat to gain the energy to live.*

1. *False. Carnivores only eat meat.*

4. *True. Plants make sugars from the carbon dioxide in the air and water from the soil.*

MINIBEASTS

This section will help you learn about minibeasts. Think about where minibeasts live and how they behave when you see them in the home or outside.

There are eight main topics in this section:

- How minibeasts develop
- Moths and butterflies
- Minibeasts that live in water
- Predators and how animals avoid them
- Which minibeasts are helpful and which are harmful
- Social insects such as bees and wasps
- How to keep worms and look at snails
- How to help and look after minibeasts

Use the symbols below to help you identify the three kinds of practical activities in this book.

EXPERIMENTS

TRICKS

THINGS TO MAKE

Introduction

In many legends beasts are ugly and frightening creatures. So what is a minibeast? Mini means small. Minibeasts are small creatures like snails, woodlice, spiders and snails. Many of them we do not notice because they are so tiny and well hidden. Others we might find ugly and frightening. Three out of every four animals in the world is a minibeast and some of them are helpful to us in very important ways. Others can be harmful or even dangerous.

Minibeasts are invertebrates – unlike birds and fish and mammals they have no backbone. Many are insects, which have a miraculous way of changing their shape and form up to four times in their life.

Minibeasts are very adaptable. They can live on land, in water and in the air, in deserts and on mountain peaks. Wherever you live there will be minibeasts. As you carry out the experiments in this section you will learn more about the many different kinds of minibeasts living all around you.

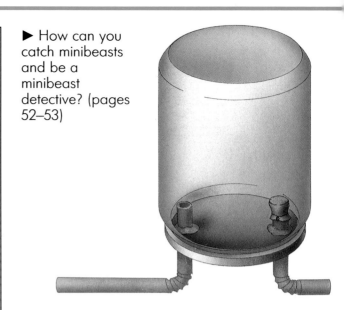

▶ How can you catch minibeasts and be a minibeast detective? (pages 52–53)

◀ What is metamorphosis? How can you keep caterpillars and watch them change into butterflies and moths? (pages 58–59)

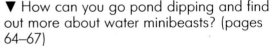
▼ How can you go pond dipping and find out more about water minibeasts? (pages 64–67)

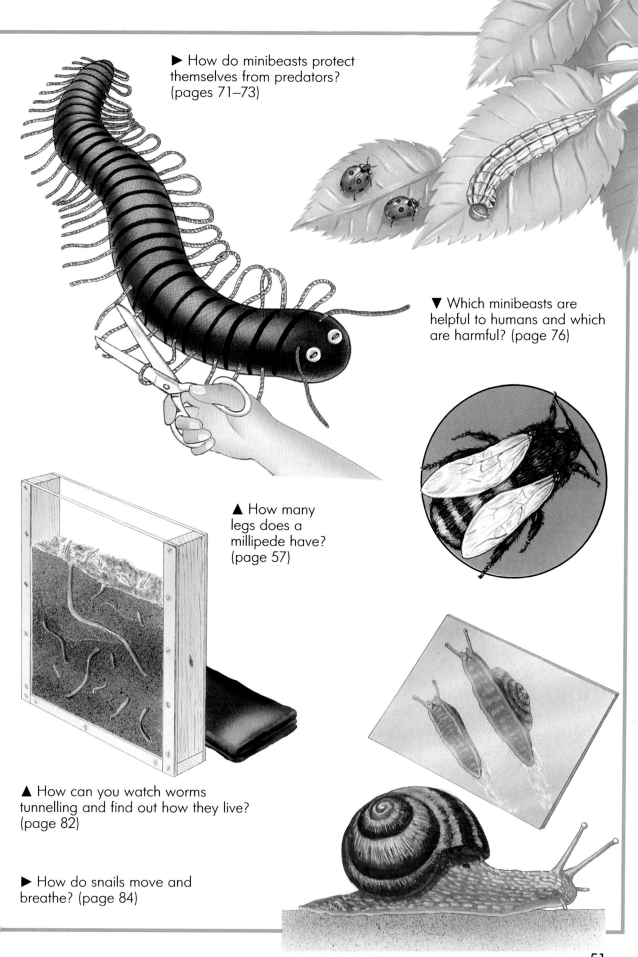

► How do minibeasts protect themselves from predators? (pages 71–73)

▼ Which minibeasts are helpful to humans and which are harmful? (page 76)

▲ How many legs does a millipede have? (page 57)

▲ How can you watch worms tunnelling and find out how they live? (page 82)

► How do snails move and breathe? (page 84)

Looking for Minibeasts

Minibeasts are all around us but can be hard to find as they are small and often hidden. Look in corners, cupboards, sheds and garages. Some live outside in long grass, bushes, trees or in the air or water. Many minibeasts only come out at night, so you may have to set traps for them.

Make a Pooter

A pooter is for catching minibeasts which are too small to pick up with your fingers. Find a small plastic container about 5 centimetres high and 4 centimetres across. Pierce two holes big enough to put a straw through in the lid. You need two wide, bendy straws. Put one bendy straw into each hole and seal the end with blu-tack or margarine. Tape a small piece of muslin over one of the straws to stop creatures being sucked into your mouth!

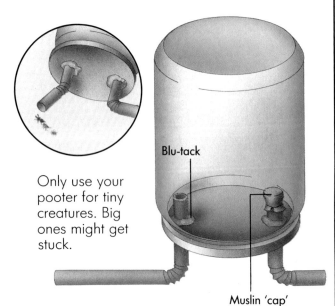

Only use your pooter for tiny creatures. Big ones might get stuck.

Blu-tack

Muslin 'cap' held on with tape

Make a Pitfall Trap

Equipment: margarine tub, stones 1–2 centimetres wide, piece of wood or cardboard, trowel.

Dig a small hole in the ground just deeper than your tub. Lay the tub in the ground and make sure the edges don't stick up. Find some stones about 2 centimetres high and put one stone at each corner. Place the wood on top to stop the rain getting in. Put some leaves and earth in the tub for the creatures to shelter in. Put in some small scraps, apple, lettuce, cheese, or tomato to attract your minibeasts.

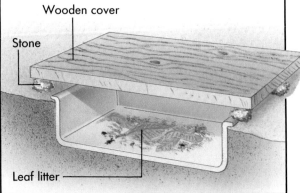

Wooden cover

Stone

Leaf litter

Be a Minibeast Detective

Using your pooter and pitfall traps try to find different minibeasts. Use a large plastic pot or tub to keep your creatures in. Remember to make your tub as similar to their natural habitat as possible. Only keep your minibeasts for one day as they will need food and proper shelter. When you have found some creatures be a minibeast detective: use these questions and a magnifier to help you find out about your minibeast. Record your findings in a notebook.

Head

Is the head large or small? Which way does it move? Does it have eyes? Where are they? Does your minibeast have **antennae** or feelers? It uses these to detect smell as we use our noses. Many minibeasts breathe through tiny holes in the sides of their body case called **spiracles**.

Wings

How many wings are there? Can you describe how it flies? (Darting, flapping, in straight line, up and down.)

Legs

How many legs does it have? Are they jointed like yours? (Your leg has a joint at the hip, the knee and the ankle.)

Where Does It Live?

Does your minibeast live in long grass, in short grass, under stones, in trees, on plants or flowers, in water, in dead wood?

Body

What colour and shape is the body? How many body parts are there? Is it **segmented** (in more than one piece)? Does the body change shape when it moves? Is it symmetrical?

Put the big creatures into the tub gently using your fingers.

Be Kind to Minibeasts

Be very careful with your minibeasts. They are very fragile. Remember you are like a giant to them!

Where Do Minibeasts Live?

Not all people like to live in a variety of places. Some people hate the heat of the sun while other people hate the rain and the damp. Some people prefer to live alone and other people like to live in families or with friends. The next section looks at which minibeasts like to live in which places.

Habitat Survey

To find out whether minibeasts like living in different places you can do a habitat survey. A **habitat** is the place where something likes to live. A snail's habitat is a cool, damp place among leaves and soil. Take a notebook and a pencil and draw a line down the middle. In the left-hand column write the different sorts of places you can look in. Start with these: in the air, in long grass, in short grass, in trees or bushes, under stones, in water, on plants, in dead leaves, in soil, in dead wood.

▲ Many insects and other minibeasts live in urban habitats. Flies feed off our food and can spread many diseases as they move from place to place.

Every time you find a minibeast put a tick in the right-hand column next to the place where you found it. Instead of a tick you might like to draw a tiny picture of the creature to remind yourself what it looked like. If you find new habitats add them to your list.

Try doing the survey on a warm, sunny day and then on a cloudy, damp day and see if you get different results.

Warning: When you do your habitat survey on minibeasts remember that if you lift a stone or piece of wood you are lifting the roof off a minibeast's home! Remember to put it back!

Exploring Woodlice

Humans can choose where they live: in towns or the country, in dry places or damp places. These experiments show whether woodlice have favourite places to live too. Divide the tub into two halves using a thin strip of cardboard (2 centimetres high). Fill the tub with soil just over 2 centimetres high.

Sprinkle/spray a small amount of water onto the soil in one half to make it damp. Collect some woodlice and put them into the middle of the tub and see which side of the tub they prefer. Half cover a tub of fresh soil with newspapers and repeat the experiment to see if they prefer light or shade.

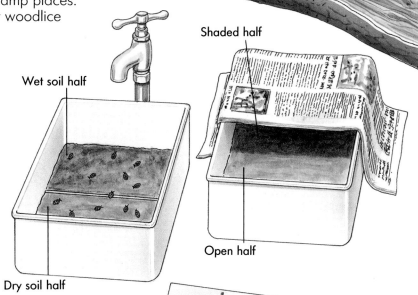

Wet soil half

Dry soil half

Shaded half

Open half

What Do Minibeasts Like Best?

Equipment: two pieces of wood, flat stone or brick.

Place the wood in a quiet corner of the garden, one piece raised 2 centimetres off the ground with stones and the other one lying flat. Make a chart as shown, drawing the creatures you find in the left-hand column. Check under the wood every day. Put one tick for each minibeast you find on the day that you find it. If you find two identical creatures put two ticks.

Your chart will help you work out which minibeasts like living alone and which in groups, and which live under tight and which under loose covers.

Tick chart

DAY	1	2	3	4

Insects and You

Some minibeasts have many things in common. If you find a minibeast with three parts to its body (*see Ant Game*), six jointed legs and two antennae then it is an insect. Most insects have wings like butterflies, bees and flies. Fleas and lice do not need to fly and have no wings; they live off the blood in animals' bodies. They are called **parasites**.

Do you have anything in common with an insect? You don't look the same but you both have jointed legs and one pair of eyes. Can you think of five other things you have in common?

Human

Your skeleton is inside your body (**endoskeleton**), while an insect has a hard outer layer (**exoskeleton**). You have warm blood, but an insect's temperature changes with the outside temperature.

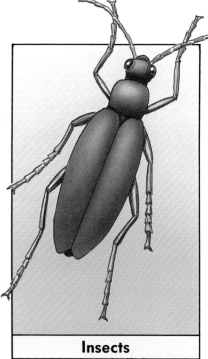

Insects

Are you the same size? Do you have antennae? What do you use to feel? Because your body is different from an insect's body you live in a different way.

The Ant Game

Equipment: plasticine, matches, dice.

If you play with a friend take it in turns to throw the dice. You must start by throwing a 1 for the head. Roll a small ball of plasticine about 1 centimetre across for the head. You must now shake a 2 for the thorax or a 6 for each antenna (you need two). Join these to the head.

Once you have the thorax you need to shake a 3 for the abdomen and a 4 for each of the legs. To make the legs you must bend a match in two places so it breaks but is still hinged.

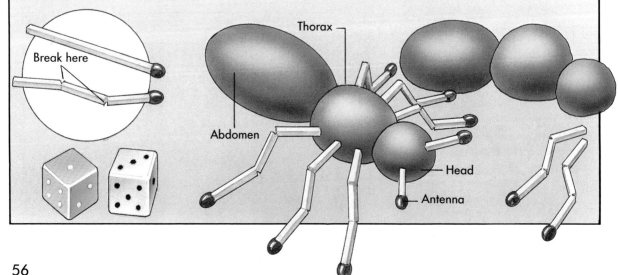

Break here

Thorax

Abdomen

Head

Antenna

Is Your Minibeast an Insect?

Go out with your collecting kit (see *page 4*) and try to find out which minibeasts are insects. Sort them into three tubs, one for insects, one for minibeasts and one for unknowns. Some insects are tricky to identify. They hide their wings by tucking them under their hard outer case. Beetles and ladybirds do this. It can also be difficult to count the number of body parts as the thorax and abdomen are often **segmented**. You may want to find a book on insects to help you.

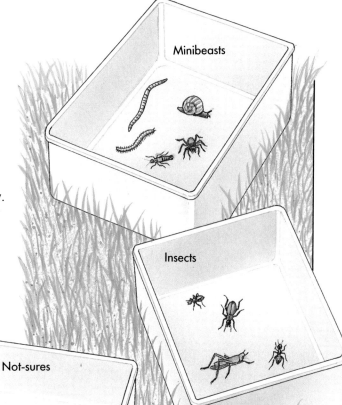

Minibeasts

Insects

Not-sures

Make a Millipede

Stuff your stocking or tight leg with filling, then sew the end up. Divide your millipede into 48 segments and thread a long piece of wool (2 metres) once through each segment. Leave a loop on each side to make the legs. Use a pipe cleaner to make two antennae.

Millipede is Latin for 1000 feet. If you count them you will see they do not really have that many.

Find a real millipede. Watch its legs ripple as it moves. The hard plates on its back are for protection and it will curl up if attacked. It can also produce a nasty smelling liquid to discourage its enemies.

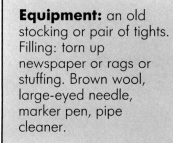

Equipment: an old stocking or pair of tights. Filling: torn up newspaper or rags or stuffing. Brown wool, large-eyed needle, marker pen, pipe cleaner.

Segmented body

Woollen legs

Cut here

Metamorphosis

Humans begin life as eggs inside their mother and are born as a small version of their parents. As they grow, the bones, muscles, skin and all the parts of their body grow with them. If you had a scar on your body as a baby it would grow bigger as your body grew. Look on your shoulder for the scar from your injections as a baby.

Minibeast Metamorphosis

Some minibeasts hatch from eggs as tiny copies of their parents too. Snails, worms, and woodlice are all like this. Other minibeasts can completely change their shape and form as they grow. They begin life as an egg laid by the female. This egg hatches into a **larva**, or **caterpillar**. The larva changes into a **pupa** and the pupa changes into the adult. This process is called **metamorphosis**. Metamorphosis is a Greek word that means 'change in shape'.

Each different stage in metamorphosis performs a different function. The job of the adult is to mate and lay eggs. The job of the egg is to store information in order to grow into a new insect.

The job of the larva is to eat and grow. The pupa is a safe case inside which the larva turns into an adult.

Egg

Larva

1. Bee 2. Ant
3. Beetle 4. Butterfly

Pupa

Adult

Keeping Caterpillars

Look for eggs and caterpillars in the spring or the summer. You will find them on grasses and the leaves of plants, bushes and trees. Oak trees and nettles are good places to investigate.

You can keep the caterpillars in a container. A big sweet jar with holes in the lid or a cake tin with an acetate (cling film) 'lid' are suitable. Cut a circle of acetate to make the lid and use tape to join this to the container.

Food Plants

Look for different kinds or species of caterpillar feeding on different plants. You must collect the right plant for the caterpillars to feed on or they will die. Some good ones to find are nettle, ragwort and cabbage.

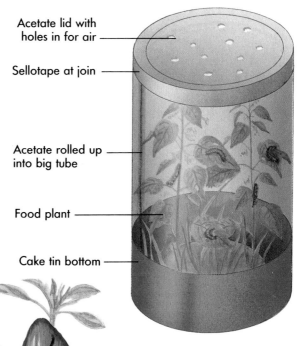

Acetate lid with holes in for air

Sellotape at join

Acetate rolled up into big tube

Food plant

Cake tin bottom

Eggs laid on underside of leaf

Pupa hanging from plant stem

Butterfly Gardening

You can attract more butterflies to your garden by planting nectar-rich shrubs and flowers. Most butterflies prefer pink, mauve or purple flowers. Buddleia, honeysuckle, lilac, cotoneaster, sweet william, marigold, cowslip and rock rose are all good. Newly born caterpillars have a soft skin which quickly hardens. As the caterpillar eats and grows the hard skin splits and the new soft-skinned caterpillar crawls out. This happens four times. Look for old skins shed by your caterpillar.

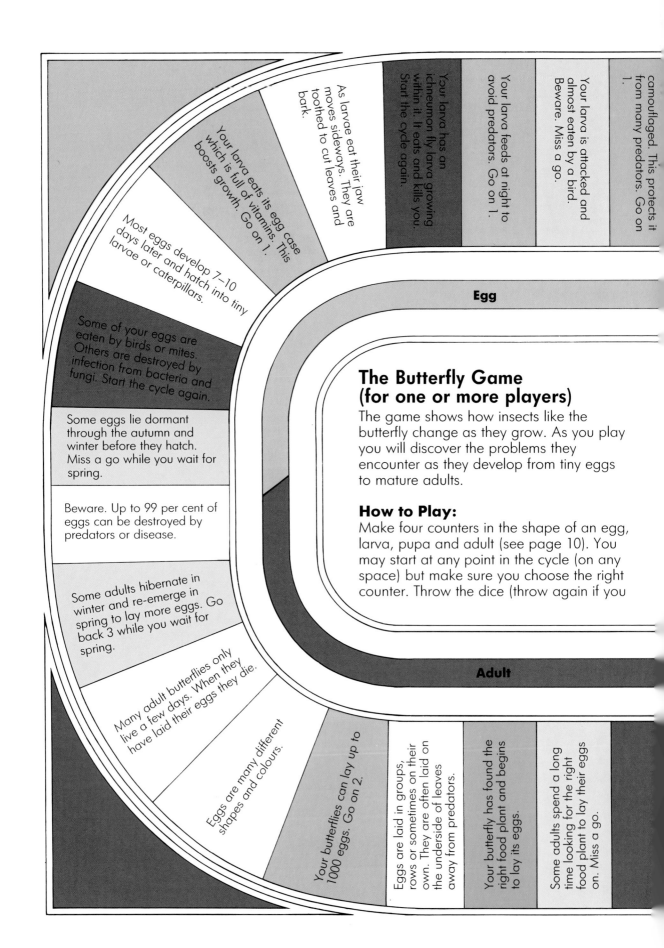

camouflaged. This protects it from many predators. Go on 1.

Your larva is attacked and almost eaten by a bird. Beware. Miss a go.

Your larva feeds at night to avoid predators. Go on 1.

Your larva has an ichneumon fly larva growing within it. It eats and kills you. Start the cycle again.

As larvae eat their jaw moves sideways. They are toothed to cut leaves and bark.

Your larva eats its egg case which is full of vitamins. This boosts growth. Go on 1.

Most eggs develop 7–10 days later and hatch into tiny larvae or caterpillars.

Some of your eggs are eaten by birds or mites. Others are destroyed by infection from bacteria and fungi. Start the cycle again.

Some eggs lie dormant through the autumn and winter before they hatch. Miss a go while you wait for spring.

Beware. Up to 99 per cent of eggs can be destroyed by predators or disease.

Some adults hibernate in winter and re-emerge in spring to lay more eggs. Go back 3 while you wait for spring.

Many adult butterflies only live a few days. When they have laid their eggs they die.

Eggs are many different shapes and colours.

Your butterflies can lay up to 1000 eggs. Go on 2.

Eggs are laid in groups, rows or sometimes on their own. They are often laid on the underside of leaves away from predators.

Your butterfly has found the right food plant and begins to lay its eggs.

Some adults spend a long time looking for the right food plant to lay their eggs on. Miss a go.

Egg

Adult

The Butterfly Game
(for one or more players)

The game shows how insects like the butterfly change as they grow. As you play you will discover the problems they encounter as they develop from tiny eggs to mature adults.

How to Play:

Make four counters in the shape of an egg, larva, pupa and adult (see page 10). You may start at any point in the cycle (on any space) but make sure you choose the right counter. Throw the dice (throw again if you

Hairs and cells on your caterpillar's face that detect the correct food plant are damaged. Go back 1.

Caterpillars have many claspers with hooks to grip onto plant stems and move from leaf to leaf.

Some larva are brightly coloured and warn attacking birds that they are poisonous. Go on 1.

As a larva grows it sheds its skin four times. The new skin is soft and allows growth to continue before it dries and becomes hard.

Your butterfly is caught by a human and killed to be put in his collection. The cycle...

Your food plant is sprayed with insecticide too. Start the cycle again.

Your larva has absorbed enough nutrients (food) and is ready to turn into a pupa.

They hang from a leaf or stem.

Some larvae spin silky cocoons around their body. Others form a pupa or chrysalis, to protect them.

Some pupae are camouflaged, spined or toughened for protection. Go on 1.

Some pupae curl up in leaf litter or soil to pupate in safety.

Cells inside the pupa move about as if in a thick 'body soup'. They rearrange themselves forming the parts of the new adult body.

Some insects hibernate as pupa in winter and emerge in spring. Miss a go while you wait for spring.

Warm weather stimulates the adult to emerge.

Larva

get 5 or 6 as these don't count). If you land on a blue space it is an advantage.

If you land on a yellow space it is a disadvantage.

If you land on a pink space your creature is killed, it is the end of the cycle and you must start again. You must land exactly on all green squares. On some of these you can change your counter.,

Butterflies encounter many dangers during their short lives. You must try and complete the cycle without being killed.

Pupa

...in his collection. The cycle ends. Start again.

The warm weather returns. Adult butterflies are mating.

The weather is cold and cloudy. Butterflies need sun to fly. Your butterfly is resting on a plant stem and cannot feed. Miss a go.

The weather is warm and sunny. Butterflies are on the wing feeding on nectar from flowers.

Your new adult butterfly takes a few hours to dry its delicate wings. It is very vulnerable to predators. Beware. Miss a go.

Moths and Butterflies

Both moths and butterflies are insects which start life as an egg. They then change to a caterpillar, then to a pupa and finally to an adult (*see page 58*). Because they are both insects they have many things in common. They both have three parts to their bodies, two pairs of wings, six legs and antennae.

Wings folded away while resting from body

Butterflies

Butterflies only fly by day. Their wings trap the Sun's warmth to give the energy to fly. Some have large 'eyes' on their wings which make the butterflies look larger than they really are which can make predators think before eating them. You can tell butterflies from moths when they are at rest. Butterflies' antennae always have knobs on the ends and butterflies hold their wings erect over their bodies when resting.

Butterflies Feeding

The caterpillar stage has powerful chewing mouthparts whilst the adult butterfly has only sucking mouthparts and lives off nectar. It uses its long proboscis to suck nectar from the base of flowers. As it does this pollen, from the stamen, sticks to its legs and is passed on to the female parts of the next flower that the butterflies visits.

Butterfly collecting Nectar

Be a Nectar Collector

Many butterflies and moths feed off nectar from flowers, and are often attracted to the flowers by their smells. Go around your garden and smell each different flower. Are the smells all the same? Can you describe them? Collect petals from the flowers you like and make a nectar cocktail.

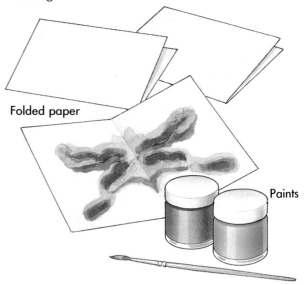

Folded paper

Paints

Symmetrical Butterfly Wings

Using a brush, put large blobs of different coloured paint onto one side of a piece of paper. Fold the clean half down onto the coloured half, smooth it with your hand, then open the paper. The image is symmetrical and can often look like butterfly wings.

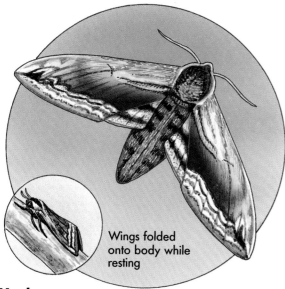

Wings folded onto body while resting

Moths

Moths get all the energy they need to fly from the food they eat. They fly, and eat, at night so do not need bright colours to attract each other. Instead the female gives off a strong smell which can attract males from a great distance. Moths usually come in dull colours which provide camouflage against their normal surroundings, making it hard for predators to find them.

Catching Moths

Moths have fragile wings, so if you catch one handle it very carefully. Put a tub with a saucer of sugar solution inside (one teaspoon sugar mixed with one tablespoon water) next to a lamp. The moths will fly towards the light, and may go to the sugar to feed.

Moths navigate using the light of the Moon, and always keep light to the same side of them when they fly. This is why they fly in circles around your lamp.

Saucer of sugar solution in box

Male moths attracted to female moths

After Dark

Wrap a piece of muslin over your tub of moths. Young female moths give off **pheromones** which a male moth can smell several kilometres away. If you attract moths to your tub then you must have some females.

Water Minibeasts

On this page you can find out about some of the creatures that live in water. Some spend only part of their life under water, while some live all their lives under water. Some can breathe under water using gills. Others need to come to the surface to breathe air.

Fold material over wire and sew

Poke wire into end of stick

Going Pond Dipping

To make a net, bend a piece of wire 60 centimetres long into a circle and push the ends into the cane, then tape it up. Fold the open end of one foot of the tights over the wire and sew it together.

When you go dipping take a large plastic tub to put your creatures in. Remember they need water! Don't pick them up with your hands as it is easy to squash them. Instead you can turn your net inside out into the tub and let the creatures swim off. Try dipping in different places: ponds, streams, ditches, rain tubs and even puddles are good places to investigate.

Water boatmen swim freely all around the pond. They are called boatmen because they use their legs like oars of a boat. Some eat plants and some are carnivorous. Look for those that swim on their back and others that swim on their front. They are insects and can fly.

Daphnia are very small. They swim by waving their feelers in the water and feed by filtering even tinier things from the water.

Water flea or daphnia magnified

Great diving beetle

Harlequin larva

Snails Snails eat dead plants and animals, and slime or algae growing in the water. They crawl along the bottom of ponds but can also move hanging down from the surface of the water.

A Different Life Cycle

A dragonfly spends the first two years of its life under water. Unlike a butterfly the dragonfly has only three stages in its metamorphosis (*see page 58*), egg, **nymph** (*see photo*) and adult. It drops its eggs in the water or lays them on water plants. These hatch into tiny nymphs which are carnivorous and feed off other creatures. They have a tough outside skin which does not stretch. Eventually it splits, uncovering a new and larger skin. Dragonfly nymphs shed their skins or moult seven times before they are ready to emerge as adults.

Mosquito and midge larva swim by flicking and twisting suddenly in the water. They are different colours, some are red (blood worms), some are transparent. Soon they turn into pupae, which hang from the surface of the water by tiny breathing tubes.

Water skater

—— Water boatman

Warning: Deep water is very dangerous. Do not go dipping in big rivers.

Caddis fly larva

—— Pond snail

maggot ——

Make a Dragonfly

Use the picture to help you with the details. Blow up the balloon and tie at one end. Do not blow it up too tight as you now need to twist it twice to form the three parts of the body. Use string or tape to hold in the twisted parts. Cover the balloon with papier mâché. To make this tear up newspapers from top to bottom into strips 2–3 centimetres wide and about 20–30 centimetres long. Work on a sheet of newspaper. Paste glue onto one strip at a time, then wrap the strip onto the balloon until it is covered. Then put at least three more layers on to make it strong. Leave it to dry. When dry, paint the body. Use the photo to help you.

Make the wings from wire bent to shape and covered with muslin or tracing paper. Glue this down at the edges. Draw on the veins. Attach them using wire wrapped round the body and twisted together underneath. Use pipe cleaners or wire for the legs. Glue these to the side of the thorax. To make the body blow up the balloon and tie pieces of string around it at the points shown to achieve a waist. Paint the body in bright dragonfly colours. To make the eyes cut a ping-pong ball in half and glue them to the head. Paint them to look like dragonfly eyes.

Equipment: long balloon, sticky paste (flour and water or wallpaper paste), pipe cleaners, newspaper, wire, ping-pong ball.

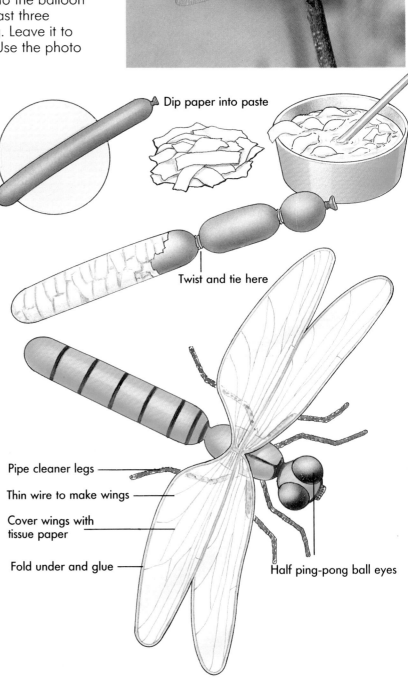

Dip paper into paste

Twist and tie here

Pipe cleaner legs

Thin wire to make wings

Cover wings with tissue paper

Fold under and glue

Half ping-pong ball eyes

Frogs and Toads

April and May are the best times to look for frogs' or toads' spawn. Collect some and watch it change. Look in boggy areas, ditches and ponds. Only take a handful as frogs and toads are getting rare. You will need a large tank or tub with water plants to provide food and oxygen for the tadpoles (they take in oxygen from water through their **gills**). About five weeks after they have emerged they need to eat protein – cheese or bacon or natural sources of protein like mosquito larvae or other small water creatures. Watch how the legs start growing and the gills disappear at this stage. After 12 weeks the froglets are fully formed.

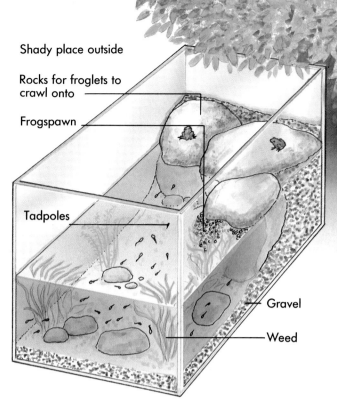

Shady place outside

Rocks for froglets to crawl onto

Frogspawn

Tadpoles

Gravel

Weed

Make a Pond

Dig a hole in the ground about 50 centimetres deep and 1 metre across, and shape it so it's narrower at the bottom. Line it with 6 centimetres of sand or newspaper then cover this with a sheet of plastic large enough to overlap the edges of the pond. Fill the pond with water then pile rocks onto the edge of the plastic sheet to keep it firm.

You can buy pond plants from garden centres or perhaps take them from another nearby pond. Stock the pond with creatures from a friend's pond or wait to see what comes to yours.

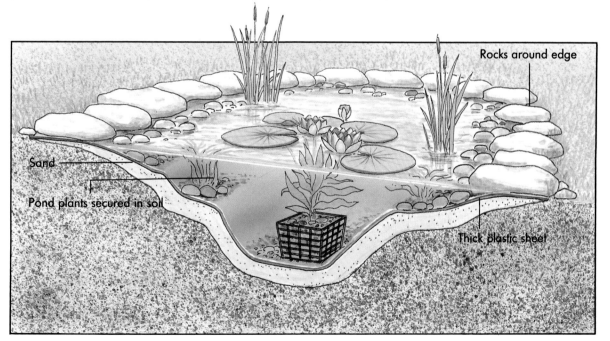

Rocks around edge

Sand

Pond plants secured in soil

Thick plastic sheet

Predators and Prey

Some minibeasts eat plants and are called **herbivores**. Some eat other creatures; they are known as **carnivores**. If a minibeast eats other minibeasts it is called a **predator**. The creature that is eaten is called the **prey**. The spider is a carnivore. It is a predator on many small insects.

Spider's Web

Spiders are able to produce a string of very fine silk from spinnerets in their abdomen. They use this silk for many purposes, though the most important is web building. The spider has developed one of the most sophisticated ways of trapping small animals. Although it looks very flimsy, one piece of silk is only 0.03 millimetres across yet is stronger than steel of the same thickness. Not all spiders make webs. Some live by catching their prey by more normal methods such as going hunting and pouncing on them unexpectedly.

Making a Spider's Web

There is more than one kind of spider's web, but the most common is the circular, or near circular type built by the garden spider. These webs are most noticeable in the autumn when they are likely to be covered in dew. Sometimes the spider sits in the centre of the web, at other times it sits beside the web, though in touch using a single silk thread, which twitches if anything disturbs the web. This type of web is never perfectly circular because the spider never finds perfectly spaced supports. The diagrams below show the major stages in building such a web. If you have a spider, give it some twigs and see how long it takes to build a web.

First the spider attaches the outer frame of the web to a convenient wall, or branch.

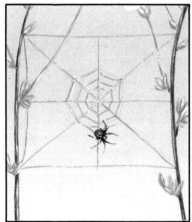
After crossing the centre with diagonals, silk is woven in spirals from the centre.

The spider reaches the outer boundary of the web. It is now complete and ready for use.

The Garden Spider Builds a Web

Stage 1. The spider lets a thread float from (1) to (2). The thread sticks when it touches a leaf or twig. The spider then joins the thread to other twigs and makes a five-sided frame.

Stage 2. The spider goes back along its first thread and makes a second loop of silk. It then drops down, leaving a 'V' shape behind. The bottom of the V makes the centre of the web. The spider spins more silk to make 'spokes' in the web.

Stage 3. The spider spins a wide spiral from the centre towards the frame.

Stage 4. The spider spins a spiral of sticky thread going from the outside to the centre. As it spins the sticky thread it eats the dry thread.

The Web Game

Making a Web

Use the pictures on page 20 to help you spin your own web. Find a forked branch of a tree with about 1 metre between the two branches. Make the web outside or bring a dead branch inside. Use string for the frame. Knot the string at points 1, 2, 3, 4 and 5, and back to 1 to make a five-sided frame. Cut, then tie on at point 6 and drop to 5. Cut. Cross from point 7 to 8. Cut. Make two diagonals from 1 to 3 and 2 to 4. Now work using thin sellotape as if this were your sticky silk. Work from the centre out towards the frame. Fold tape over in the centre to hold it fast. Move from the centre to the first string (a). Press the string hard onto the tape, spiralling outwards until you reach the frame. The sticky side of the tape should always face the same way.

Preparing the Game

First make six flowers for your branch. Cut up an egg box and stick six tissue paper petals around the cup. With a drawing pin stick flowers to the branch around the web, cups facing up. Now make ten hoverflies. Crush a small piece of tissue paper into a body shape 2 centimetres long. Wrap it in sellotape. Cut tissue paper wings and stick them onto the middle of the body.

'Cup' flowers

Sticky-tape web

Forked branch

Playing the Game

Hoverflies feed off nectar from flowers. The spider is one of their predators. Throw your hoverfly gently towards a flower in the hope that it will land there to feed. If it lands on the floor you may try again (three chances). If it does not get nectar food by then it will die of exhaustion. If it gets caught in the web you can try to free it. If you tear its wings it is dead. How long can your hoverflies survive?

Spiders Without Webs

Not all spiders make webs. Many are hunters and pounce on their prey. The wolf spider has powerful fangs, injects poison into its victim and then sucks its body dry. Because it has no web it carries its eggs in a sac underneath its body.

Catch a Web

Equipment: card, talcum powder, glue.

Spiders' webs are extremely delicate and any attempts to preserve them have to be carried out with the utmost care. Great patience and some delicacy is required. The principal difficulty is that spiders' webs are difficult to see, before and after you have preserved them.

The first thing to do is find a spider's web, preferably one hanging in an open space. So that the spider's web will be easier to see blow some talcum powder over the web. It should cover the web in a fine even layer. Next, spread a layer of glue over a piece of black card and carefully bring the card up behind the web. The object is to stick the web to the card without changing its shape, so push the card against the web very gently.

▲ A spider's web. The silk used is stronger than steel.

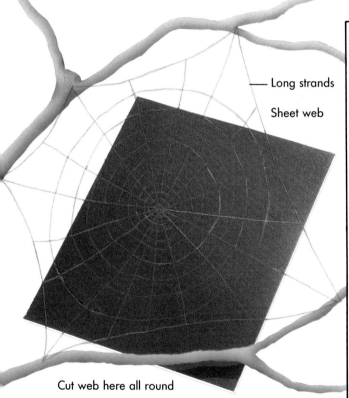

Long strands

Sheet web

Cut web here all round

Cut the web around the card so that it is no longer attached to its original supports.

To preserve the web cover it with sticky-back plastic or spray it with varnish.

Money Spiders

Money spider webs are everywhere. Look in and around hedges. The web is not sticky but small creatures fall into the long strands then drop to the ground. The spiders hang in wait underneath, quickly catch their prey, then wrap them in silk for storage.

Money spider hangs in wait

Money spiders spin webs all year round but they are particularly common in the autumn. At this time of year there may be as many as one million in an area the size of half a football pitch and money spiders trap millions of insects each year.

Colour and Camouflage

All living things need some way of protecting themselves. A wasp can sting, a snail can hide in its shell, a spider can run. A caterpillar has no sting, no shell and cannot move fast, so it protects itself by **camouflaging** its body. This means its body is the same colour or shape as the things around it.

Does Camouflage Work?

Look through old magazines and cut out pictures with different colours — green, brown, red, blue, yellow, pink, orange. Cut out pieces of these colours about 3 centimetres square and stick onto cardboard. You will need about eight of each colour. For two players give half the cards to each person. Place them around the garden, in trees, on leaves and grass. Do not hide them but place them where they can be seen. Now see how many pieces you can find in five minutes. Look for your friend's pieces first and then your own. You will find that the most difficult to see are those that match the background colour most closely. There are five camouflaged minibeasts hidden in the picture above. See if you can spot them.

Disguise a Caddis

A caddis fly spends most of its year-long life under water as a larva. To protect itself the larva builds a camouflaged case around its body. Make a caddis case using a thin cardboard tube. Close the tube at one end with tape and cover it all with glue. Cover your case with natural materials. Make your caddis from plasticine and put it in the case.

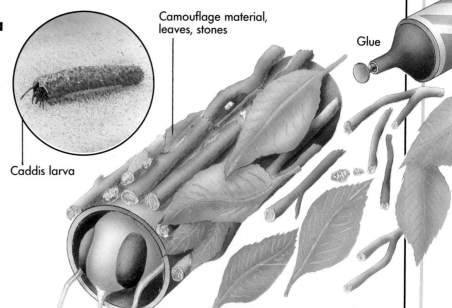

Caddis larva

Camouflage material, leaves, stones

Glue

71

Means of Protection

Different minibeasts have different ways of protecting themselves. This illustration shows you some examples. On your next minibeast hunt check to see if they work. There are five minibeasts on this page that are protected because they are camouflaged. Can you find them?

Minibeast Enemies

The most common enemies of minibeasts are lizards, mice and birds. Both moles and badgers eat mostly worms and when other food is hard to find foxes and badgers will often eat beetles. Guess which animals might eat the different minibeasts in this picture.

Butterfly

Caterpillar

Earwig

Millipede

Grasshopper

Woodlice

Snails and Slugs
Snails have a shell and can retreat or hide in it to protect themselves. Slugs are covered in mucous which makes it difficult for birds to pick them up.

Caterpillars
Many caterpillars camouflage themselves to hide from predators. Others have bright colours and patterns to warn the birds that they are poisonous.

Crickets and Grasshoppers
Grasshoppers and crickets protect themselves using camouflage. They can also jump very suddenly to escape danger. They can jump up to 1 metre high, which is 40 times their height.

Worms

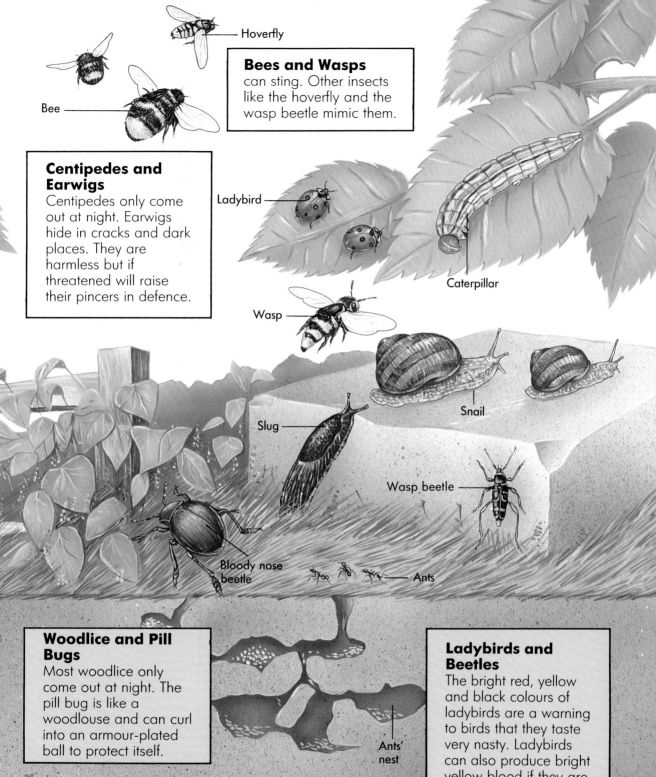

Hoverfly

Bees and Wasps
can sting. Other insects
like the hoverfly and the
wasp beetle mimic them.

Bee

**Centipedes and
Earwigs**
Centipedes only come
out at night. Earwigs
hide in cracks and dark
places. They are
harmless but if
threatened will raise
their pincers in defence.

Ladybird

Caterpillar

Wasp

Snail

Slug

Wasp beetle

Bloody nose
beetle

Ants

**Woodlice and Pill
Bugs**
Most woodlice only
come out at night. The
pill bug is like a
woodlouse and can curl
into an armour-plated
ball to protect itself.

**Ladybirds and
Beetles**
The bright red, yellow
and black colours of
ladybirds are a warning
to birds that they taste
very nasty. Ladybirds
can also produce bright
yellow blood if they are
frightened, which can
put off their enemy. The
bloody nose beetle uses
this method of defence
and produces bright red
blood from its mouth or
leg.

Ants'
nest

Ants and Worms
Both ants and worms
live in tunnels. They
come to the surface for
food.

Watch that Warning (Game)

Cut out ten circles of paper about 5 centimetres across. Colour five with warning colours and patterns and the other five with camouflage colours and patterns. Use the creatures illustrated here and on pages 24 and 25 to help you. Tape a peppercorn to the back of the warning cards and a jelly baby to the back of the camouflage cards. Spread the ten cards on the grass, colour facing up. Each card is a juicy minibeast. Tell your friend to be a hungry bird. They must choose which ones to eat without knowing what is on the back. When they have chosen one they must bite into and taste the food on the back. See how long it takes them to learn which minibeasts taste good and which taste bad.

Use of Colours

For various reasons insects are many different colours. Some use their colours to hide, others to show up more clearly. The bright, coloured ones use colour and pattern to recognise each other. The insects above use colour to warn predators that they are poisonous.

Make a Giant Ladybird

Equipment: Newspaper, paste, balloon, paint.

Cover a round balloon with papier mâché (see page 66). Leave it to dry overnight and then cut the balloon shape in half. Mark on your ladybird's head, thorax and wing cases and then paint its bright warning colours. Use one of the pictures to help you. Sellotape on some pipe cleaner legs. You can use the other half of your balloon to make a beetle or woodlouse. Using the same method and different shaped balloons you can make all sorts of model minibeasts .

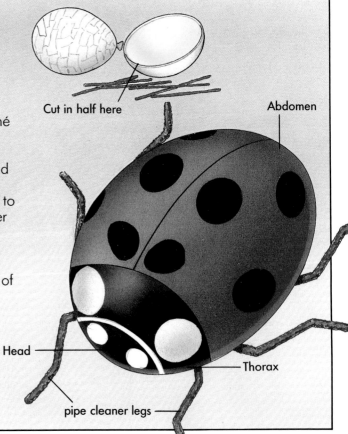

Cut in half here

Abdomen

Head

Thorax

pipe cleaner legs

Play the Ladybird Game

Equipment: eggbox, raisins, dice, paint.

Cut a square 15 × 15 centimetres. Cover with leaves. This is the board for the game and is the garden in which the minibeasts live. Paint the cups from the eggbox red with black spots. This game shows that the number of ladybirds depends on the number of aphids in the summer. One raisin = 1000 aphids.

To play: 1. Throw the dice for April. If you throw 3, put out three raisins and begin to feed one ladybird. Each ladybird needs 1000 aphids per month to survive. 2. Roll dice for May. Feed the ladybird. 3. If you have some good months you can begin to feed other ladybirds, so when you have earned five raisins spare start feeding more ladybirds. Keep feeding all the ladybirds until September. Was it a good year for the ladybirds? Playing this game shows that during years with plenty of aphids, many ladybirds survive.

Raisin-aphids

Ladybird cups

Make a Creepy Crawly Course

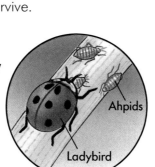

Ahpids

Ladybird

Imagine you are the size of a ladybird or ant. What would the world look like? Use a magnifying glass to find out, or a cardboard tube which makes everything bigger when you look down it. Go into the garden and crawl around looking very closely at the magic world of minibeasts. Set up a miniature assault course. Use sticks, leaves and stones to build your course, and perhaps try using a saucer of water.

Did you know Ladybird larvae are unable to sense their prey until they touch it. If they find aphids they will eat up to 15 in one day.

Ladybird, ladybird fly away home,
Your house is on fire, your children will burn . . .

Some people think this is a warning to ladybirds because in September farmers used to burn the hop fields which were full of ladybirds.

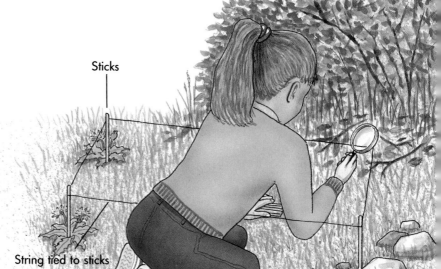

Sticks

String tied to sticks

Helpful or Harmful?

Some minibeasts are helpful to humans, some are really harmful and some are just a nuisance. Ants are a nuisance, as are the larvae of the woodworm beetles that make holes in furniture until it falls apart. In Africa swarms of locusts eat everything in their path and can strip a field of crops in a few hours. Mosquitoes, fleas and other insects carry diseases like malaria.

▲ Many insects, such as this butterfly feed from nectar in flowers. They also help fertilise other flowers.

Why Do Insects Visit Flowers?

Insects go to flowers looking for nectar. They are attracted to the flower by the bright colours and the smell or scent. Do an experiment to find out which scents and colours attract which insects.

Colour Make cards and paint them different colours. Each card should be about 30 centimetres square, yellow, red, blue, green, pink, orange or black. Lay the card squares on the grass on a warm sunny day. Find out which is the most popular colour by keeping a record of the insects that visit the cards.

Scent Insects are also attracted by scent and the knowledge that food or nectar is near.

Pick the least visited colours and add a smear of honey. Insects will now visit these colours, attracted by the smell.

Keeping records on a clipboard

	moth	bee	wasp	fly
Red	✓✓	✓		
Blue				
Yellow			✓	✓
Green		✓✓		✓
Purple	✓✓		✓	✓
				✓

Coloured card

Social Insects

Bees, wasps and ants live in colonies so can help look after each other. Some collect food, some look after young, some mate and lay eggs.

A colony of bees has about 50,000 workers, 300 males and one queen. The males' job is to try and mate with the queen who flies high into the sky, where only the strongest male can follow and mate with her. The queen's job is to lay eggs, as many as 2000 in a day.

It's a Bee's Life

Worker bee

The workers' job is to feed the growing larvae. This keeps them very busy as each larva needs about 1300 meals a day! For the first three days the workers feed them on royal jelly (a mixture of honey, pollen and a special juice from their glands). After this, if they are fed only on royal jelly they become new queens, but if their diet changes to a mixture of honey and pollen they become workers.

▲ Worker bees feeding the growing larvae. Each hexagon is a cell containing one bee larva.

When a new queen is born the old queen leaves, taking about half the colony with her. This is called swarming.
If two new queens emerge at the same time they will fight to the death. The winner will kill all other queen larvae or pupae so as to have no rivals. During the winter bees feed on honey stored in the hive but if it is cold many will die.

Worker Bee Experiment

Worker bees can carry up to half their body weight in nectar and sometimes travel 10–13 kilometres to a good patch of flowers. Weigh yourself and calculate half your body weight. Find something of that weight and try carrying it. Could you go 13 kilometres?

Workers also have to build up the winter's supply of honey. To make 500 grams of honey, bees fly 80–160 thousand kilometres. It is hardly surprising that many die of exhaustion, and it is estimated that up to 1500 die each day in a typical colony.

Travelling with a heavy load

Busy as a Bee

Your finger is the bee. Cut out wings to stick on your finger and mark stripes on the body with a felt tip pen. Visit the most brightly coloured and sweetly scented flowers you can find. Put your finger in towards the nectar at the base of the flower. Your bee is trying to feed on nectar. Go to another flower and look for more, this transports pollen which fertilises the plants. Without insects many of our food plants (fruits, vegetables, etc.) would not be fertilised.

Choose a Flower

Find a flower that is visited often by bees. Choose one bud and tie a woollen marker on it so you can find it again. For ten minutes each day watch the flower and note down how many insects visit it. There should be a day when pollen ripens and gives off the most scent and many more bees visit. Remember that on cloudy days insects are less active.

Plastic wings

Striped finger bee

Bees collecting pollen and nectar

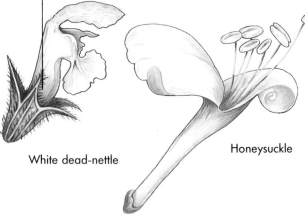

Nectar stored here

White dead-nettle

Honeysuckle

Taste the Nectar

It is possible to taste nectar from some flowers – easy ones to try are honeysuckle and white dead-nettle. Look for a flower that is fully opened. Pull gently from the plant, bite off 1 millimetre at the end and suck.

Did you know? A worker bee has a barbed sting at the end of its abdomen. If it uses its sting it will die as the tip of its abdomen is ripped out. The male bees or drones can't sting, but beware! The queen bee can sting repeatedly.

Bumble Bees

Look for bumble bees. They are thicker and more hairy than honey bees. They live in colonies of about 150 bees. In autumn they all die except the new queens.

Making Bee Homes

Many of the bees and wasps we see are not from colonies like honey bees or bumble bees. They live on their own, making small nests in soil or hollowstems and holes. The female lays a few eggs in each hole and leaves a stock of pollen and nectar as food for the new larvae. She then dies and the new bees appear the following spring.

Make some homes for solitary bees and wasps. Plug one end of each straw with plasticine or cotton wool. Put them in a tin can or attach them under a window sill in a warm sunny place.

Use strong tape or wire to attach the bunches of straws to the windowsill.

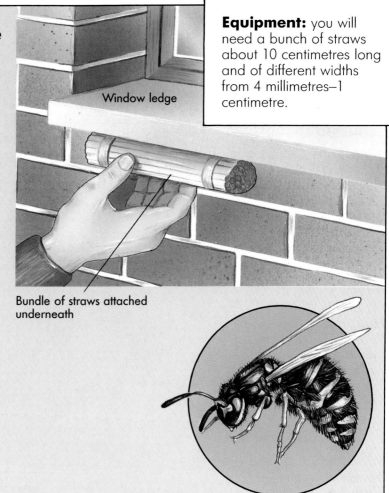

Window ledge

Bundle of straws attached underneath

Equipment: you will need a bunch of straws about 10 centimetres long and of different widths from 4 millimetres–1 centimetre.

Wasps

Wasps also live in social colonies like bees. There are usually about 2000 wasps in each colony. In spring wasps are busy collecting food for their hungry larvae. They use their sting to kill small insects like aphids and caterpillars. The larvae produce a sweet saliva that feeds the wasps until they are all hatched in late summer. Then they look for food in other places – rotting fruit or jam . Wasps are a nuisance and can be very dangerous if they sting you in the mouth or throat. The photo on the right shows a wasps' nest.

Life In the Ant Colony

Ants are social insects like bees and wasps. The different members of their colony have different jobs to do. First the queen rubs off bits of her wings, as she will not need them again. She then tunnels into the ground and makes a chamber where she will lay her eggs. The males' job is to mate with the queen. She raises the first worker larvae on her own. Once they have emerged, some nine months later, they will begin to run the colony for her. Workers have different jobs:

Remember: ants can sting.

some are nurses tending the young, some are cleaners, and some forage for food. The foragers feed the other workers, by passing liquid food directly into their mouths. As they do this they rear up on their legs and look as though they are kissing. This is also the way the queen passes messages to the ants in her colony. She secretes liquid 'messages' on her body that the workers lick off her and pass around the colony. They tell the ants what needs doing in the colony.

Make a Formicarium

Equipment: two sheets of perspex 25 centimetres square, one sheet 5 × 25 centimetres, three wooden battens 5 × 25 centimetres and 15 millimetres thick, screws, tape.

Screw the perspex sheets to the wooden battens as shown and attach the lid using strong tape. Make sure they fit tightly to prevent the ants escaping. Look for black ants to fill the formicarium under garden paths and flat stones or yellow ants in grassy mounds. When you find the nest dig down to try and find the queen, who is much bigger than the workers. Put as many workers as possible into the formicarium with the queen. Gently fill the formicarium with enough soft earth to cover the ants, so fill it about three-quarters full. Place some of the following food in with them: ripe fruit, seeds and small scraps of cheese or jam. Occasionally spray the soil with water to give the ants something to drink.

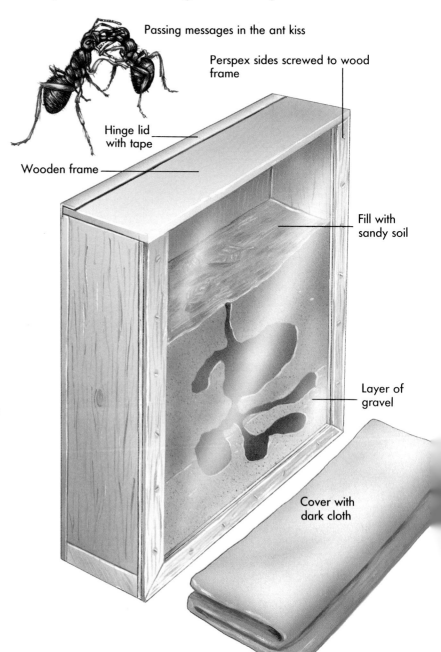

Passing messages in the ant kiss

Perspex sides screwed to wood frame

Hinge lid with tape

Wooden frame

Fill with sandy soil

Layer of gravel

Cover with dark cloth

Ant Safari

You may be able to find ant colonies thriving in the garden. A favourite place for ants to make a nest is under a large flat stone. Look under slabs in your garden. If you have any old bricks or slabs lay them out in a deserted corner of the garden and see if you can encourage an ant colony to nest there. Putting out attractive food might help. Look for ants in different stages of their life cycle. The eggs are small and white, the larvae are white maggots and the pupae are like tiny beans.

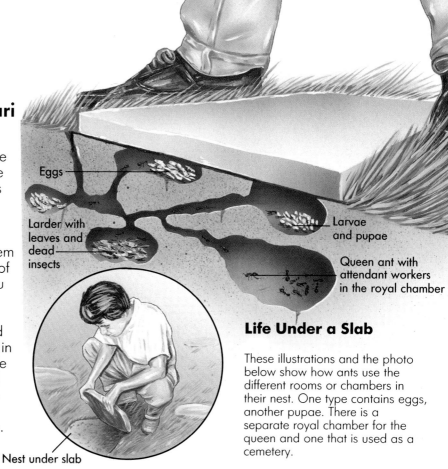

Eggs

Larder with leaves and dead insects

Larvae and pupae

Queen ant with attendant workers in the royal chamber

Nest under slab

Life Under a Slab

These illustrations and the photo below show how ants use the different rooms or chambers in their nest. One type contains eggs, another pupae. There is a separate royal chamber for the queen and one that is used as a cemetery.

How Worms Help

Worms tunnel beneath the soil. Their tunnels can reach a depth of 1.5 metres. Worms eat their way through the soil in search of dead plant material. The matter that passes through them is pushed towards the surface where it forms worm casts. With two million worms living in an area the size of a football pitch a huge amount of earth can be shifted.

Worm Dances

Worms usually only come to the surface at night when they are not in danger of being eaten. Some birds have a way of tricking them to the surface by tapping or pecking at the ground. If the soil is damp you can entice them to the surface by doing a worm dance: gently stamp your feet, making sure you don't keep moving them or you might tread on the worms. Continue for about five minutes or until worms start popping up.

Make a Wormery

Make your wormery the same as the formicarium (see p. 80). Put in different layers of stones and soil, with 5 centimetres gravel at the bottom. Put in two or three layers of different coloured, moist, soil. The different layers will enable you to see how worms help to move soil about. Make sure you keep a layer of leaves or grass cuttings on the surface. Watch how they pull these down into the burrows. Both ends of a worm look similar, but on closer inspection you will see that one end, the head, is more pointed than the other.

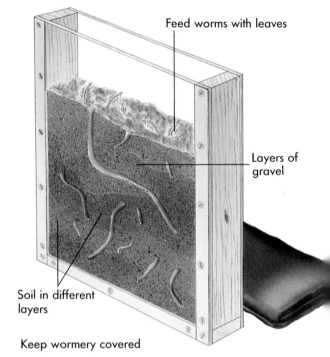

Feed worms with leaves

Layers of gravel

Soil in different layers

Keep wormery covered

You may see some worms with a thick band around the middle of their body. This is where they store their eggs. The belt or saddle gradually moves down the body and eventually drops off, forming a protective **cocoon** around the eggs.

Muscular segments stretch and contract

Saddle, contains eggs

Bristles

Worm Experiments

Listen to the bristles

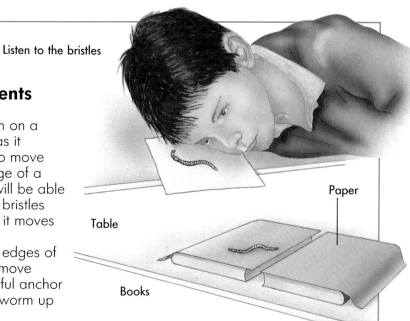

Paper

Table

Books

Listening to worms: Put a worm on a piece of moist paper and watch it as it contracts and spreads its muscles to move forward. Hold the paper on the edge of a table and put your ear close. You will be able to hear the scratching sound of the bristles underneath its body that grip when it moves along.

These bristles grip the soil on the edges of the burrows and help the worm to move forward. They can also make a useful anchor if a hungry bird is trying to pull the worm up out of the ground.

Bridging the gap: Put two books on the table. lay a sheet of paper on each but leave a gap of 3 centimetres between the two sheets. Sprinkle water on one sheet so it is damp. Put your worm on the dry sheet and watch it 'bridge the gap' to get to the wet sheet.

This shows that worms prefer damp places, so you should always keep the soil in your wormery damp.

Other Worms

There are many millions of earthworms constantly tunnelling beneath the soil. There are also many types of earthworm, of varying sizes, which live in a wide range of habitats some preferring rotting material like compost, for example the red and orange brandling worm. There are also many types of smaller worm which are not the same family as earthworms and are normally too small to find with the naked eye.

Worm Watching

Measure out 1 square metre on an open piece of grass. If you can find an area with worm casts so much the better, as this is a sign that worms are already active. Pin down some different worm foods under a piece of fine netting (old net curtain works well). Try different leaves and small bits of fruit or vegetable. Make a map, marking where you have put everything. Come back each morning to see if anything has gone.

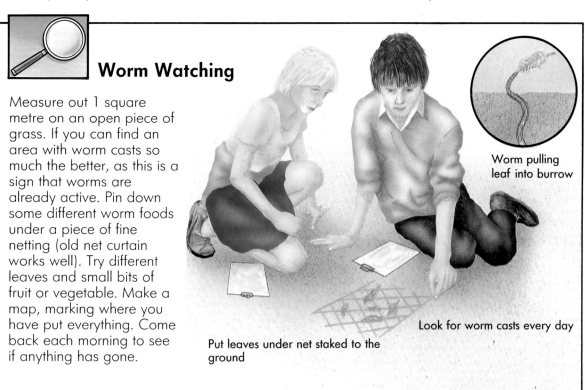

Worm pulling leaf into burrow

Look for worm casts every day

Put leaves under net staked to the ground

Snail Watching

Snails try to avoid hungry predators by only coming out at night. This also stops them drying up in the sun. If it is too hot or too cold the snail can shut its door and seal the entrance to its shell with a layer of hard mucous.

Most snails eat plants but some are carnivores and eat other small creatures. Snails are **hermaphrodite**. This means they have both male and female parts to their body. When mating the snails stick together and shoot a 'love dart' carrying sperm into the other snail. They can then both lay eggs.

Shell

Feelers or antennae

Breathing hole

Foot

Put your snail on a sheet of stiff clear plastic. Wait till it has come out of its shell and started exploring. Turn the plastic upside down and watch the rippling muscles of the snail's foot as it moves along. A snail leaves a trail of slime as it moves. This is important to help it to slide over rough or sharp objects.

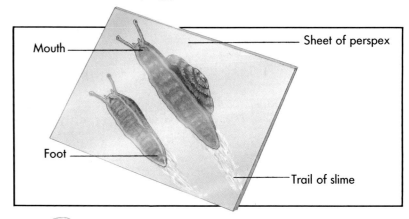

Mouth

Sheet of perspex

Foot

Trail of slime

Garden snail

Edible snail

White-lipped snail

Anvil stone

Broken shells

Do Snails Have a Home?

A snail carries its home, its shell, on its back. Leave an old flower pot or margarine tub on its side in a damp place in the leafy undergrowth. Check daily to see if snails visit. If you get a visitor paint a red spot on its shell and see if it returns.

Different Shells

A snail's shell is very important. It stops the soft body from drying out. If it is very hot in summer or cold in winter the snail can seal the entrance of the shell with a layer of hard mucous. As the snail grows the shell is enlarged from the entrance.

Snail Snacks

Snails make a tasty meal for any bird that can open their shell. The song thrush is very good at this. It bashes the snail against a hard stone to crack the shell. Around where this has happened you will find pieces of broken snail shells.

Developing Multi-storey Minibeast Homes

Find a quiet corner of a garden where you can make your own minibeast housing development. You will need to let the grass and wild flowers grow so check that this is all right with whoever looks after the garden. Use all the ideas in this book to help you provide homes for as many creatures as possible. To encourage butterflies to the top storey of your high open-air garden let the grass and nettles grow and plant some wild flowers (*see page 59*). To encourage

basement tenants leave some bricks and slabs about. Pile some old bricks, flower pots and bits of wood or piping to provide hidden nooks and crannies for those that live on middle storeys. Put out bits of food like vegetables, leaves and pieces of fruit to encourage ground floor dwellers. An old rotting log is an excellent addition, providing secluded rooms and facilities for many species. An old flat bowl dug into the ground and filled with water encourages those creatures that prefer to spend their time under water. Caring developers will check regularly that their tenants are happy and that facilities are maintained to standard.

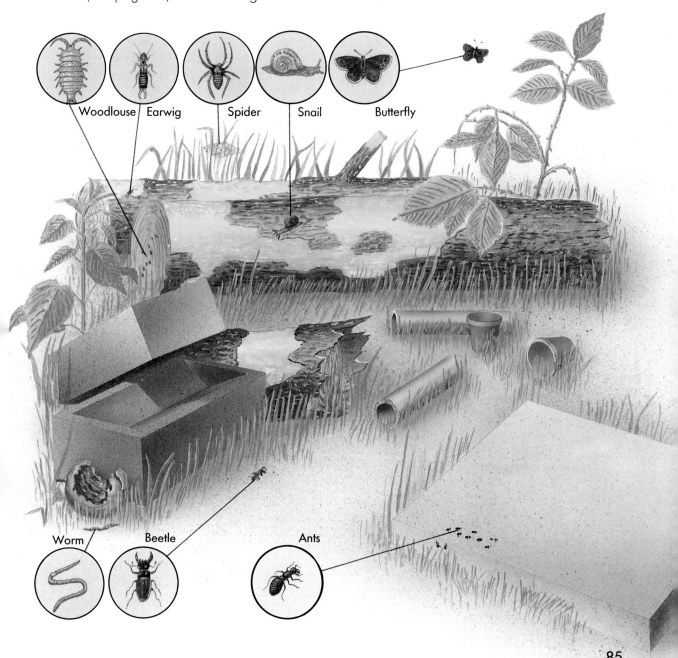

Woodlouse   Earwig   Spider   Snail   Butterfly

Worm   Beetle   Ants

Make a Minibeast Meadow Frieze

Equipment: grasses, plants, paints, white wax crayon, large sheet of white paper.

To make the background to your meadow draw lots of thick vertical lines like grass shadows down the page. Mix up a watery pale green or blue paint and brush this over the wax. The thin paint will not colour the waxed areas.

Paint one side of your grasses and plants, then press them gently against your meadow picture to make a print. Cut out and stick on bright coloured tissue paper shapes to make flowers. Your meadow is now ready to be filled with minibeasts. Make careful drawings by sketching outside from real life. Sometimes if you look on window ledges, you can find dead minibeasts, as well.

A Mini-Visitors' Book

Many people keep visitors' books and record the dates and activities of their visiting guests. Record the visits you get from minibeasts where you live. Make one book for inside guests and one for outside guests. Record what they do on their visits, the date when they arrive, and the date they leave.

Prints of grasses and flowers in the meadow

Helping Out

Minibeasts are useful to us in many ways. There is an enormous amount of matter locked in the chemical structure of all living things. When they die this can be released and returned to the earth and used again by plants to make more sugars. Minibeasts contribute to this by feeding off the remains of dead animals and breaking down the materials within. Smaller micro organisms such as bacteria further this process and return much of the chemicals in dead organic matter to the soil.

Dead mouse

Skin is rolled off

Beetle drags mouse underground

Sexton Beetles

These are some of the larger beetles that help recycle dead animals and plants. The beetle digs a hole under carcass, and then pulls it into the hole. As this happens the skin is rolled off the body. Eggs are laid in the hole and the flesh provides food for the larvae.

Dor beetle making dung ball

Dor Beetle

The dor beetle is also called a dung beetle. It digs a burrow up to 60 centimetres deep and buries a ball of dung there for its larvae to eat. This helps to fertilise the soil.

Vital Cleaners

Place a small dead animal or bird in a plastic container or margarine tub with holes pierced in it. Fill the container with soil, seal with a lid and bury it 20 centimetres under the ground. Mark the spot where you buried it. Dig it up four weeks later. The fleshy parts of your creature will have been consumed by mini- and micro-beasts in the soil. Extract the skeleton carefully and you may be able to reassemble it.

Lid

Plastic container

Soil

Holes in container

Dead mouse

Minibeasts Quiz

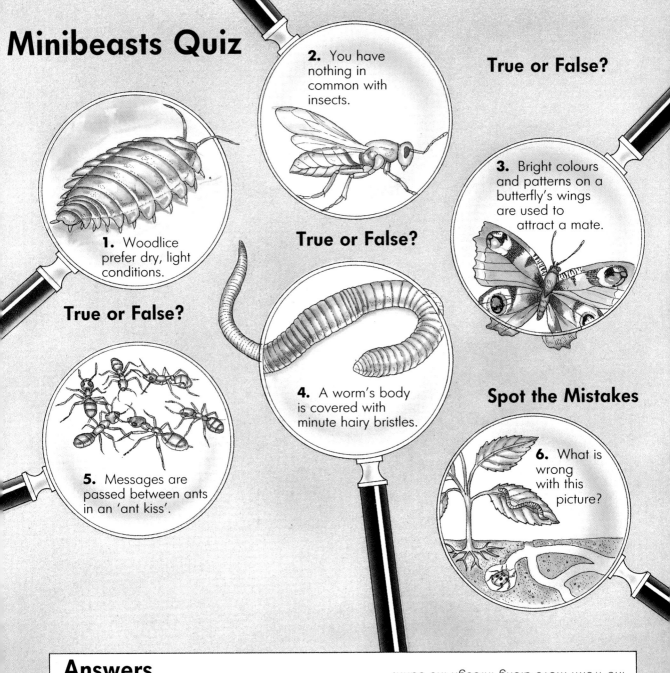

2. You have nothing in common with insects.

True or False?

1. Woodlice prefer dry, light conditions.

3. Bright colours and patterns on a butterfly's wings are used to attract a mate.

True or False?

True or False?

4. A worm's body is covered with minute hairy bristles.

Spot the Mistakes

5. Messages are passed between ants in an 'ant kiss'.

6. What is wrong with this picture?

Answers

1. *False. Wood lice like to live in damp, dark places, under stones and in rotting wood.*

2. *False. Both you and an insect have a head, eyes, jointed legs, and moving bodies, and you both breathe oxygen. There are also many differences.*

3. *True. The bright colours are usually on the male to help attract a female. Some patterns, like large eyes, serve to frighten away attackers.*

4. *True. These bristles grip the soil and help the worm move along through the earth.*

5. *True. The queen ant secretes liquid messages on her body. The workers lick these off and pass them on to other ants via an "ant kiss."*

6. *Earthworms do not climb on plants, and ladybirds do not live underground.*

TREES AND LEAVES

This section of the book will help you learn about trees.
Think about trees when you see wooden furniture and write
on paper and when you go for a walk in the countryside.

There are seven main topics in this section:

- What a tree is made of
- How a tree grows
- Leaves and why they fall
- How trees reproduce
- The animals that live in trees
- How wood is used
- Saving the great forests

Use the symbols below to help you
identify the three kinds of practical
activities in this book.

EXPERIMENTS

TRICKS

THINGS TO MAKE

Introduction

Trees are the largest living things in the world. Some, such as the giant redwood can reach heights of 110 metres. Though tall they are not the biggest trees. That record goes to a particular Californian sequonia which is 83 metres high and 24 metres around the trunk. If uprooted it would weigh 2145 tonnes. Though to us trees seem like giants they are closely related to small garden plants which we dwarf. Like all plants trees can convert sunlight into food. In doing so they change carbon dioxide from the atmosphere into sugars for their growth and release oxygen which animals breathe. For this reason the great rain forests, where millions of trees are found, have been called the 'lungs of the planet'.

Five thousand years ago nearly three-quarters of the world's land area was covered by trees. Today between 70 and 90 per cent of these have been cut down and huge areas are cut down every minute. An area of trees acts as an air purifier, a power station, and a housing complex. Clearing these areas makes people homeless, kills the animals living there and ultimately affects our ability to survive.

▶ How can you find out how old or how high a tree is? (page 93)

▼ How many different types of leaf are there and how do they work? (pages 102–109)

▼ Where do trees come from and how do they reproduce? (page 110)

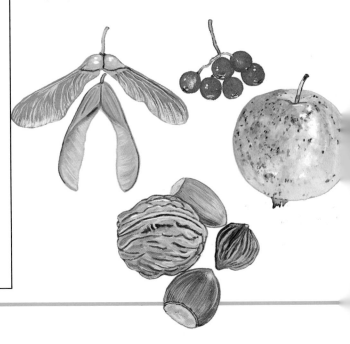

▲ How does a twig tell its own history, and what is inside a bud? (page 101)

▲ How do trees grow and how can squirrels damage them so easily? (page 99)

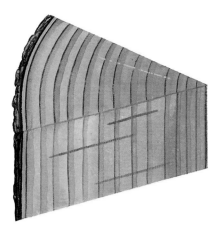

▲ How do trees grow? (page 98)

▼ How can you preserve leaves to keep them as a record? (page 106)

▲ Why does a tree have leaves and why do they change colour and fall? (page 108)

▼ Where do fruits and seeds come from and why are they important? (page 114)

What Is a Tree?

Plants are different from other living things because they can use sunlight to make food and grow. To reach the light plants have evolved tall thin stems. Trees are different from other plants because they have a tough woody stem. Look at the trees growing in gardens, parks and woods near you. They are very exciting when you find out how they work.

Where Does Your Tree Live?
This tree is called 'Crinkle Leaf'. Its address is 50 Paces From the Back Door, Near the Shed, Back Garden.

Be a Tree Estate Agent
Choose a tree that is in a garden, park, field or wood near you. We shall now try to help you discover how your tree is special and why it is important. Just as estate agents advertise for sale houses for people to live in, so you can be a tree estate agent by making a poster to advertise your tree and encourage creatures to come and live there. (For trees are homes for many, many creatures.)

Tree Fingers
You need a small mirror. Stand at the edge of your tree and hold the mirror flat with one end on your nose. Look down into the mirror. You should be able to see the twigs of your tree. The little twigs are like the tree's 'fingers' stretching into the sky. Follow one finger in towards its arm (branch) and then to its shoulder (where it joins the trunk).

Stand about 30 paces from your tree and draw it. But first look very carefully at it. Notice how each branch splits and divides from the trunk to the finger tips.

How Old Is Your Tree?

Use a piece of string (or tape measure) to measure the **girth** (the distance around the middle) of your tree. It is most accurate if you measure it at about 1 metre high.

Every 2.5 centimetres around the girth corresponds to about one year in a tree's growth.

Work out the area covered by the branches of your trees. Walk from the trunk to the edge of the crown in eight different directions. Draw this using 1 centimetre for one pace. Join these so you can see the shape of the crown. Use your diagram to work out the area of the crown.

How High Is Your Tree?

Stand about 15 paces from your tree. Hold a pencil at arms length and line up the bottom of the pencil with the base of the tree. Gradually walk backwards away from the tree until the tip of the pencil is lined up with the top of the tree. The point on the ground that lines up with the end of the pencil is the place the top of the tree would land if it fell over. Pace out this distance to find out how tall the tree is.

Pencil

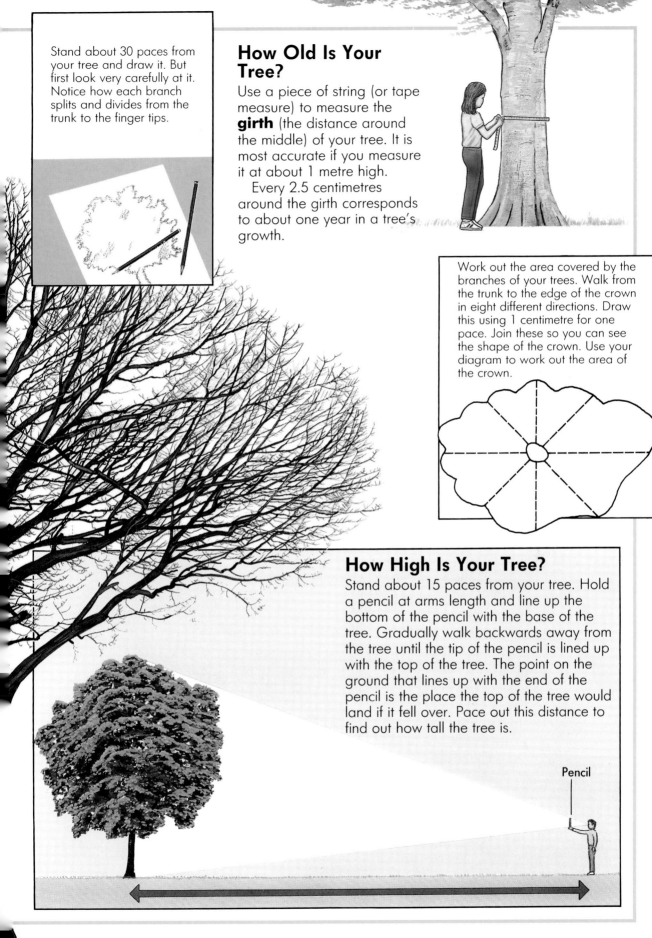

Make a Tree Poster

Make a tree poster like the one shown here, and use it to record what you find out about your tree.

Tree name Crinkle Leaf

Address 50 Paces from the Back Door, Near the Shed, Back Garden.

Age The foundations of this tree were built over 60 years ago and it has been growing ever since.

Roots Six sturdy feet (roots) provide firm foundations.

Bark Makes good thick walls to protect the inside of the tree. Tiny slits (lenticels) in the bark provide an air-conditioning system, letting air in and out.

Branches provide attractive old style timber structure for the upper storeys making light, airy rooms available at all levels.

Twigs make stairs for smaller residents to climb to upper storeys. Buds make upward extensions of the home, providing new rooms each year.

Buds and new leaves provide a constant supply of free meals for some residents (minibeasts, birds) and visitors (deer).

Leaves These are furnished rooms with meals provided for smaller tenants such as leaf miners.

Crown This tree has 25 square metres of crown area. This offers spacious roof-top balconies and gardens with excellent views.

Flowers and seeds Flowers from some trees (apple, horse chestnut) provide meals for visiting bees and butterflies. Seeds from our tree (acorns) provide food for squirrels.

Environmentally friendly This tree is environmentally friendly. Leaves produce oxygen. They also reduce the amount of carbon dioxide in the air.

Bonus Our tree has its own sound system. Sounds vary from the gentle sounds of the wind to the noisy music of birds chattering.

Further bonus Free decoration four times a year. Every season the tree home is redecorated. Summer colours, dark green, autumn colours, browns, red and orange, winter black and white, spring, bright green.

In the shade Dead branches are outbuildings providing further accommodation for minibeasts.

Tree Music

Sit under your tree with your eyes closed. With your hand in a fist raise one finger each time you hear a new sound. Record the sounds you hear on a cardboard 'tape' like these. Begin with your pencil on start. Go up if the noise gets louder or higher, go down if it gets softer or lower.

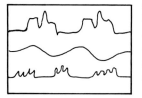

We recorded three sounds. The sound of a bird (*top*); the sound of the wind in the trees (*middle*); the sound of rustling and crunches in the leaves (*bottom*).

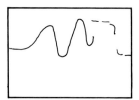

Choose one bird and try to record its song. This song rose and fell twice, followed by three high short notes and two low short notes.

Tree Scents

Every leaf has its own special scent. To discover the scent crush the leaf between your fingers until the green juice comes out. Mix the crushed leaves in a half cup of water to make a cocktail. **Remember** some leaves such as privet can be poisonous!

Crushed leaves

Shake Hands with a Tree

When people meet they often shake hands. To meet a tree you need a blindfold. Tie a scarf around a friend's head carefully, so the person cannot see. Now lead your friend to any tree in the garden. He or she must get to know every detail of the tree by feeling it. Can they reach round its girth or waist? Help them feel for lumps and bumps and special touches and textures. When your friend has found out everything about the tree take off the blindfold. Can your friend find the same tree again by feeling and using his or her eyes as well? Swap over. Get to know your own tree with a blindfold on and mark all the bumps and cracks and crevices on your poster.
Warning Be careful to guide your friend carefully so they don't trip.

Make a Tree

Roll up three sheets of newspaper into a tube 3 centimetres wide. Tape loosely. Cut down the tube as shown with wiggly or straight lines about 1–2 centimetres apart. Pull up at point (A) from the inside sheet of paper. Paint the newspaper first with thin watercolours to make coloured trees.

Equipment: Large newspaper, scissors, water colour paints, sellotape, cardboard.

Cut tubes here to make leaves

A

Make a Forest

Cut a piece of thick cardboard from a box, paint it and lay it flat. Make many trees of different heights and colours. To stand your trees up cut a finger of cardboard out from the base. Place the trunk over the finger and tape it down.

Cut tubes here to make roots

Tape roots to board

97

How Does a Tree Grow?

Trees grow in two ways. Outwards growth occurs in the cambium layer. Each year cells in this layer divide and grow. They grow outwards pushing the bark, which eventually splits and falls off and is replaced. A tree's upwards growth occurs at the tip of each twig.

Tree Transport

The inward growth of the cambium forms the main part of the trunk. This is called xylem. Much of this wood is made up of dead or dying material but it still has a very important role to play. The xylem is made of tiny tubes which transport water and minerals from the roots up the trunk and branches to the leaves. Leaves need this water to help them make food from sunlight. The outward growth is provided by a layer of phloem. This is made up of tiny tubes that transport the sugars from the leaves to the rest of the tree. The phloem is very important and if it is damaged the tree will die.

Root Hairs

Roots may not go down deep but they can spread outwards as far as the tree is tall. They have many tiny **root hairs.** These take essential moisture and minerals up into the tree. Root hairs increase the surface area of the root and increase the amount of water the tree can take up.

Branch Scar

If a branch dies, it falls off and leaves a round-shaped scar. Look for branch scars on your tree.

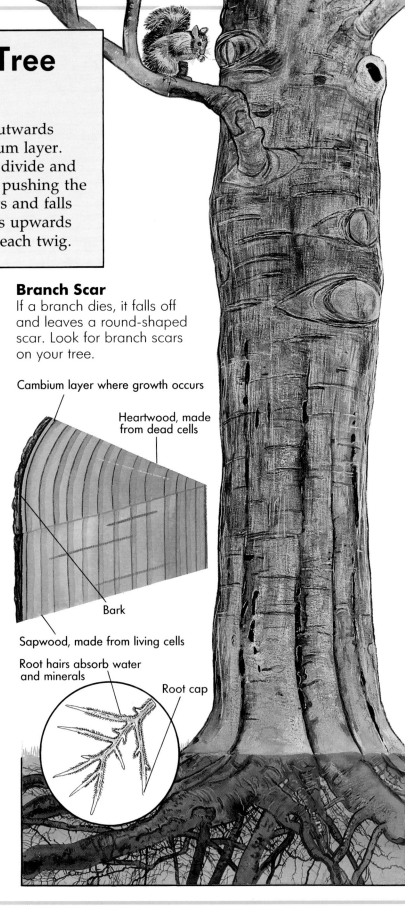

Cambium layer where growth occurs

Heartwood, made from dead cells

Bark

Sapwood, made from living cells

Root hairs absorb water and minerals

Root cap

Proving Bark Is Important

Squirrels often eat bark, especially from tender young trees and twigs. They eat the bark in a ring around the twig or trunk. This destroys the important **cambium layer**, and the tree dies. Peel off 1 centimetre of bark at the base of a small twig, as a squirrel might do to a young tree. Record what happens over the next few weeks.

Squirrels chew bark off twigs

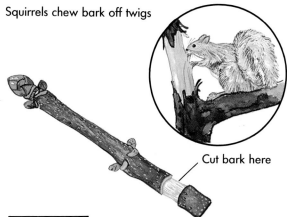

Cut bark here

Looking for Lenticels

Take a small new twig from your tree. Peel the top layer of bark off. Look for holes in it. These are partly filled with a powdery substance. This is loose cork from a cork layer under the bark. In summer these holes allow water out and air in. In winter they are sealed. As bark grows the holes or **lenticels** stretch and split sideways.

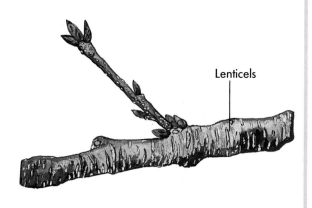

Lenticels

Weaving with Bark

Score some twigs at 10 centimetre intervals and all down one side (see below). Peel off the bark and flatten it between layers of newspaper for a few hours. Cut strips about 5 millimetres wide. Lay four strips out to start. Weave four others in the opposite direction then gradually weave in more strips until your mat is finished.

Score along these lines

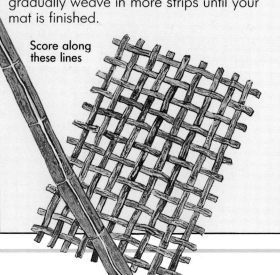

Bark Rubbing

All trees have a different bark pattern rather as people have finger prints. Record different trees' 'finger prints' using wax crayons. Is bark the same all over the tree? Do rubbings at different heights to find out. Use some to illustrate your poster.

Tie paper round trunk

Rub with crayon

Twigs and Buds

Like a branch, a twig's job is to support and transport. Twigs support the leaves which have the important job of making food. Leaves need to collect the Sun's rays to make food so they must be held up as high as possible. Twigs also transport water *to* the leaves and sugars *from* the leaves, using tiny tubes.

Tale of a Twig

Choose a twig on your tree and find out its history: look at the **girdle scars** to find out how old it is; peel off the bud scales (the protective layer around the bud), and you will find a series of rings beneath. Each year a new bud grows. When the bud scales fall off a new girdle scar is left. Count the scars and you will know how old your twig is.

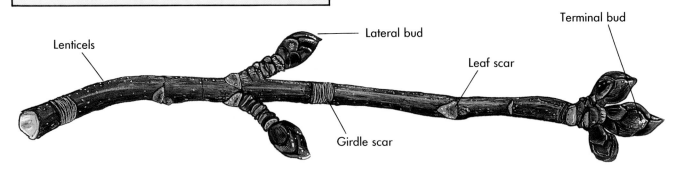

Lenticels

Lateral bud

Terminal bud

Leaf scar

Girdle scar

The shape at the end of the horse chestnut leaf is a horseshoe. Look on the twig for the **scar** left behind after the leaf fell. Can you see small dots in a semi-circle in the scar? They are the holes where the **xylem** and **phloem** tubes are.

When the bud has opened a new green twig is growing. Mark it with ballpoint pen at 2 centimetre intervals. Measure these each day to see which part of your twig grows the most.

◄ This photograph shows the open bud scales with new twigs and leaves emerging.

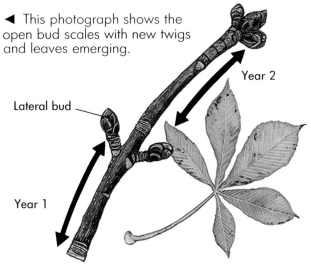

Year 2

Lateral bud

Year 1

Where Do Buds Grow Best?

Pick three small twigs with buds that are about to open. Put them in pots of water. Leave one on a warm windowsill, leave the second in the fridge and the third in a dark cupboard. Measure how much each twig grows each day. Compare the growth rates of your indoor twigs with a twig on your tree growing outside in the garden.

On warm windowsill

In a dark cupboard

In the fridge

Tag a Twig

New twigs and leaves come from the bud. See what happens when the main or **terminal** bud is knocked off. Tie some red wool round a twig growing on your tree and remove the terminal bud. Check every two days to see what happens.

Break bud here

Tie wool here

Buds and Leaves

Cut some buds in half to find out what is inside. Use large buds from different trees. Do they all look the same inside? Try opening the tiny leaves that are tucked inside. Look for tiny flowers too. Do all buds have scales on the outside? Bud scales protect the soft new leaves inside. The bud scales of the horse chestnut are sticky to protect them from hungry insects and birds.

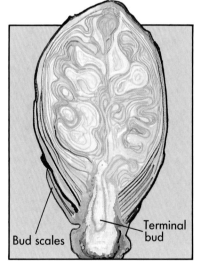

Bud scales

Terminal bud

New Leaves

Look for new leaves that have just opened out from their bud. Use these pictures to help you work out how they were packed inside.

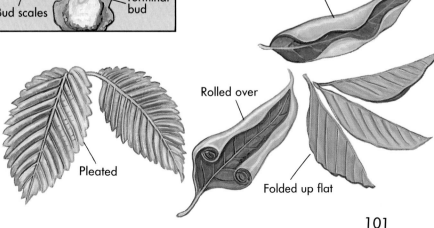

Curled up

Rolled over

Folded up flat

Pleated

Leaves

Try to imagine a world without leaves. All the trees and plants would be bare. Not only would the world look very dull (like a permanent winter scene) but humans and animals would have nothing to eat: leaves provide them with all their food because they turn sunlight into food energy. Leaves are also important as they make the oxygen in the air that we breathe.

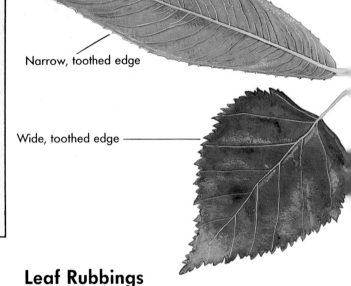

Narrow, toothed edge

Wide, toothed edge

Bags of Leaves

Collect leaves from as many different trees as you can find. Sort them into eight piles of leaves with different shapes. You will find that nearly all your leaves will be one of the eight kinds similar to the ones on these pages.

Leaf Painting

Choose some leaves with large veins or ribs. Paint the underside of the leaf with a thin layer of paint, then press the leaf carefully onto a clean, white sheet of paper. After a few seconds peel the leaf away. You will find that the shape of the leaf is painted onto the paper. Try this with different leaves.

Leaf Rubbings

Choose some leaves with large veins and ribs. Lay them upside down on a piece of paper. Lay another piece on top and hold it steady with one hand. Using the side of a wax crayon rub evenly over the leaves. The shape of the leaf will gradually emerge. Compare these to your bark rubbings.

Painting Leaf Shadows

Hold your leaf firmly on a clean sheet of paper. Dip your brush well in the paint, and make brush strokes out onto the paper from the centre of the leaf. When you have painted all round the leaf lift it off. A white shadow of your leaf remains. Make several leaf shadows on the same piece of paper and compare them. Make a collage of your leaf shadows.

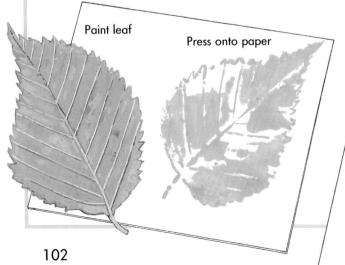

Paint leaf

Press onto paper

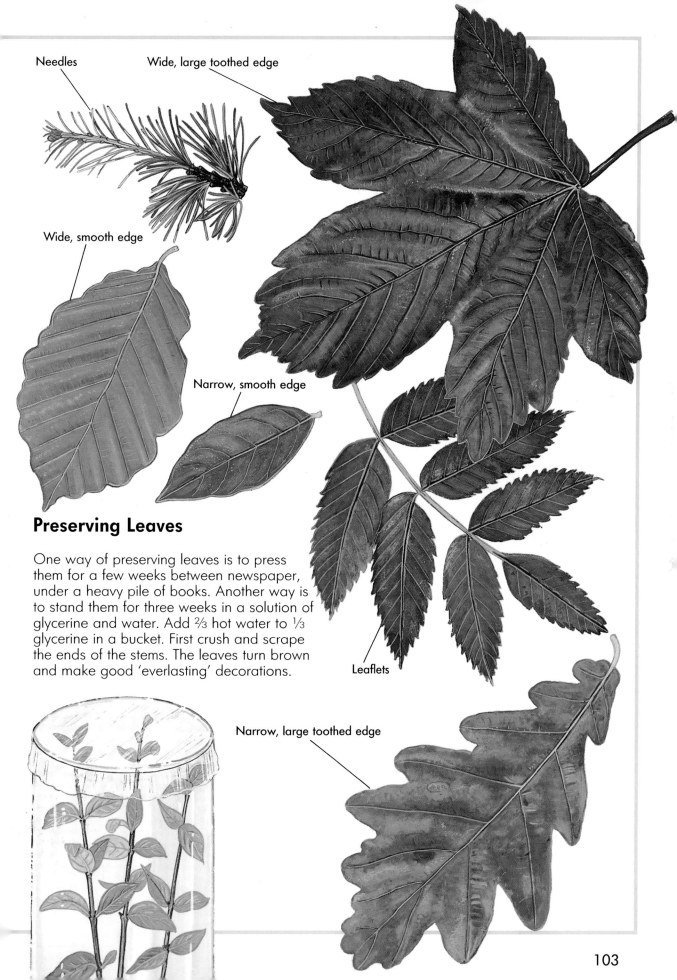

Needles

Wide, large toothed edge

Wide, smooth edge

Narrow, smooth edge

Preserving Leaves

One way of preserving leaves is to press them for a few weeks between newspaper, under a heavy pile of books. Another way is to stand them for three weeks in a solution of glycerine and water. Add ⅔ hot water to ⅓ glycerine in a bucket. First crush and scrape the ends of the stems. The leaves turn brown and make good 'everlasting' decorations.

Leaflets

Narrow, large toothed edge

A Family of Leaves

Collect lots of different leaves from the same tree. Make four piles from the smallest to the largest. Which is the most common size? Which part of the tree has big leaves and which part has smaller leaves? The leaves are different sizes because the smaller ones come from the shady areas which get less sunlight.

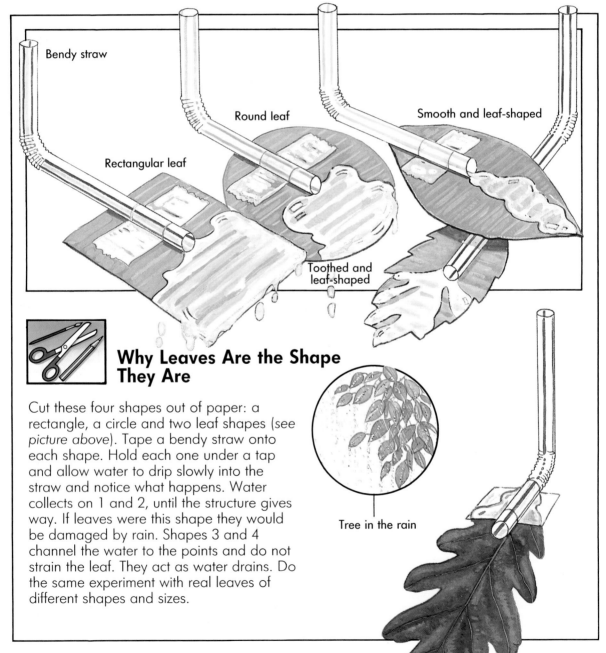

Bendy straw

Rectangular leaf

Round leaf

Smooth and leaf-shaped

Toothed and leaf-shaped

Why Leaves Are the Shape They Are

Cut these four shapes out of paper: a rectangle, a circle and two leaf shapes (see picture above). Tape a bendy straw onto each shape. Hold each one under a tap and allow water to drip slowly into the straw and notice what happens. Water collects on 1 and 2, until the structure gives way. If leaves were this shape they would be damaged by rain. Shapes 3 and 4 channel the water to the points and do not strain the leaf. They act as water drains. Do the same experiment with real leaves of different shapes and sizes.

Tree in the rain

Sun Traps and Food Producers

Leaves are like miniature food producers. They make food to help a plant or tree to survive. Humans and animals couldn't survive without these food producers either, because they live by eating them. Leaves use the Sun's energy, water, and carbon dioxide in the air to make food (sugars). They act like solar panels to trap the Sun's energy. You can see how much light they trap by holding up a sheet of white paper towards the Sun while standing near the tree's trunk. The surface will be dappled or completely covered by leaf shadows. The surface area of leaves traps nearly all the Sun's light.

▼ Looking up into a tree from underneath. Little of the sky is visible. This is because the leaves trap as much of the sunlight (energy) as they can to make food.

Sun

Sunlight + Water + Carbon dioxide
⇨
Sugars + Oxygen

Paper held near edge   Paper held near trunk

How Big Are Your Solar Panels?

Find the surface area of one leaf by drawing on a centimetre-squared grid. Put your leaf on the grid and draw round it. Estimate the area by counting 1 for each square half covered or more and 0 for each square less than half covered.

To find the total area of our tree's solar panels we estimated the number of leaves on a small twig, the number of small twigs on a small branch, the number of small branches on a large branch and the number of large branches on the trunk. Then we added it up.

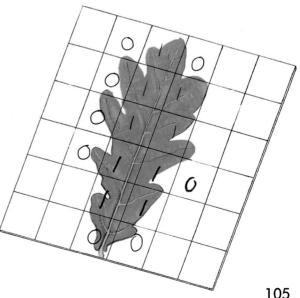

Why Trees lose Their Leaves

Leaves get worn and damaged and need to be replaced. On this page you will find out that some trees lose all their leaves at the same time, in autumn, and new leaves grow all at the same time, in spring. This kind are called **deciduous** trees. Other trees replace their leaves gradually throughout the year. They are called **evergreen** (because they always look green).

Which Side of the Leaf?

Leaves have holes in them called **stomata**. The tree loses water or **transpires** through these holes. Use two large leaves. Put vaseline on the upper side of one and the under side of the other. Vaseline will fill up the holes. Cover each leaf with a small clear plastic bag. Secure round the leaf to make it airtight. Check your leaves every hour especially if it is sunny weather. You will notice that more water is given off by the under side of the leaf. This is because it has more stomata than the upper side.

Losing Water

Trees lose water through leaves. You can prove this by picking two twigs of about the same size. Take the leaves off one twig, then put the twigs in separate pots with the *same* amount of water. Mark the water line on both pots. Put a small plastic bag round one set of leaves. Leave for a week. Check the water level every day. Notice in which pot the water goes down.

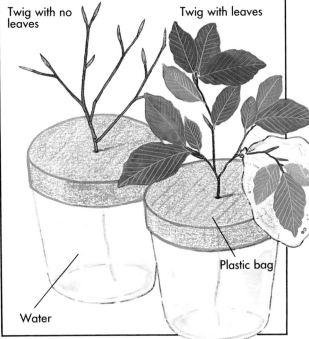

Twig with no leaves

Twig with leaves

Plastic bag

Water

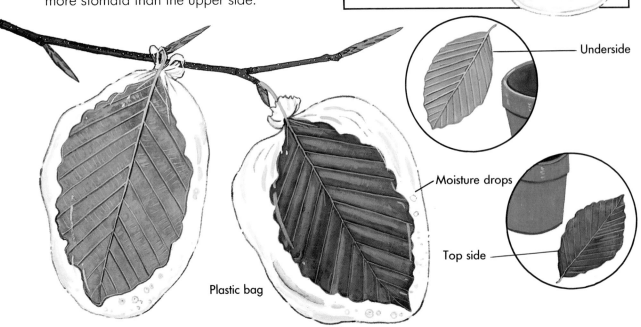

Plastic bag

Underside

Moisture drops

Top side

Deciduous and Evergreen

Trees cannot take in water through their roots in cold wintry weather. This means they would dry up or **dehydrate** if they didn't drop their leaves before winter. (Remember trees lose water – transpire – through their leaves.) Their leaves fall in autumn in preparation for the cold winter weather. But evergreens do not lose their leaves in autumn. So how is it that they don't dehydrate?

▶ Conifers have bendy branches and needle-like leaves so that snow can slip off and will not break the branches.

Investigating Evergreens

Collect a variety of evergreen leaves, holly, ivy, firs, spruce, cedar. Try the plastic bag experiment on these leaves and see what happens. Notice the hard waxy layer covering the leaf. This stops the leaf losing so much water.

Compare these with new deciduous leaves that are soft and fresh. Deciduous leaves lose water quickly and have a much greater surface area over which to lose water.

Imitating Winter

Pick a small twig of leaves. Put it in the freezer for an hour and then leave it in water for a few days and see what happens. Your leaves will be tricked into thinking winter is on the way. The deciduous ones should shrivel and fall. The shorter hours of daylight in autumn are also an important sign to trees that winter is on the way.

Holly

Scots pine

Spruce

Different evergreen leaves

What Happens to a Leaf in Autumn?

Collect a bag of autumn leaves and find out how they are changing colour. Are they changing all over from green to yellow to brown? Elm leaves do this. Do the veins change colour first or last, or does your leaf change colour irregularly in blotches? By looking at your tree find out if the largest or the smallest leaves change colour first.

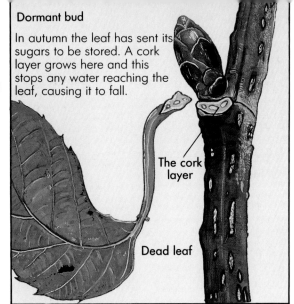

Dormant bud

In autumn the leaf has sent its sugars to be stored. A cork layer grows here and this stops any water reaching the leaf, causing it to fall.

The cork layer

Dead leaf

Colour changes around veins first

Colour changes between veins first

Colour changes in irregular blotches

Why Leaves Change Colour

Leaves have a yellow **pigment** (colouring) in them (some have red or orange pigments too). The green colour of **chlorophyll** covers up these colours. In autumn the chlorophyll drains away. The yellow and red colours are left behind.

Leaf Skeleton

Find some large leaves with clear veins and ribs. Simmer the leaves at a low heat for half an hour in plenty of water. Leave them outside in a bucket for a few weeks. Now rinse your leaves in clean water to remove the decaying 'flesh'. Dabbing them with a soft paint brush will help. You will be left with the veins of your leaf. This is called a leaf skeleton. Stick your leaf skeletons on card to make attractive greetings cards or bookmarks.

Cross a Leaf

Put some coloured or masking tape on a green leaf in the shape of a cross. Leave the leaf on the tree. If leaves can't get light they cannot make chlorophyll. After a few days you should be able to see the yellow pigment showing under the tape.

Tape over leaf

Veins

Leaf Pictures

Collect your favourite leaves. Look for special colours and shapes. Lay them flat between several sheets of newspaper and leave them under a heavy object. After about a week your leaves should be dried and pressed. You can display them by sticking them on your windows (use a dab of glue or Blu-tack). You can also make pictures by glueing them down. Try making trees, flowers, figures and abstract patterns. Pressed coloured leaves make good cards and bookmarks. Mount them on a sheet of card and cover them with sticky-backed plastic.

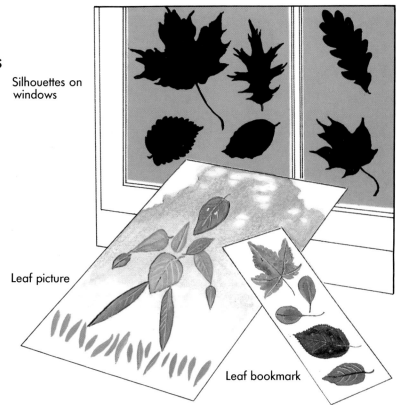

Silhouettes on windows

Leaf picture

Leaf bookmark

What Happens to Leaves?

When leaves fall in a wood they form a thick crunchy carpet. If trees drop a layer of leaves 20 centimetres deep each year, after 10 years there would be a 2-metre thick carpet of them! This doesn't happen because leaves are made of organic material (this means they were once living). When organic things die they **decompose** or rot. Put 10 leaves in a tin, leave them for four weeks, and check regularly to see what happens. Find out if all leaves decompose at the same rate: pin down various leaves under plastic netting.

Rotting leaves

Leaves under net

Where Do Trees Come From?

Animals start life as a tiny egg. Plants begin life as a small seed such as an acorn. Seeds hold all the 'growing information' for a new tree to develop but need certain conditions to **germinate** or begin growing. Once it has started growing and has its own leaves it can then use the Sun's energy to make its own food.

▲ An oak tree seedling growing out of an acorn. The root begins to grow first. This splits open the shell of the acorn. The shoot then begins to grow, using the food stored in the acorn halves.

Sorting Tree Seeds

Different trees produce different kinds of seeds. Some produce seeds in a fleshy covering – a fruit or berry; some produce seeds tucked into the folds of cones or catkins; some produce seeds with wings and others produce seeds inside a hard covering like nuts or pods.

Go for a walk and see how many seeds from trees you can find. Sort them into these six categories (kinds). Look for seeds from trees in the kitchen too (nuts and fruits).

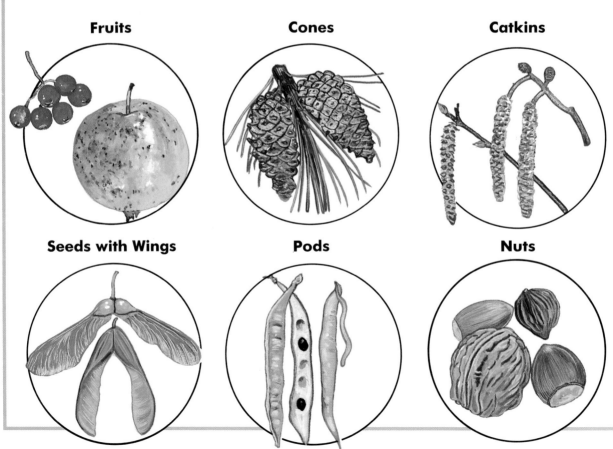

Fruits   **Cones**   **Catkins**

Seeds with Wings   **Pods**   **Nuts**

Tree Fruits In the Kitchen

Many of the fruits we eat such as apples, bananas and pears come from trees. A fruit is a fleshy wrapping for a seed. Cut up some of your kitchen fruits and see if you can find the seeds inside. Tomatoes and cucumbers are fruits too: they have seeds with a fleshy case around them. Try growing some trees from fruit seeds: orange, apple and pear seeds will sometimes grow. Start them off by putting them on a saucer with damp cotton wool.

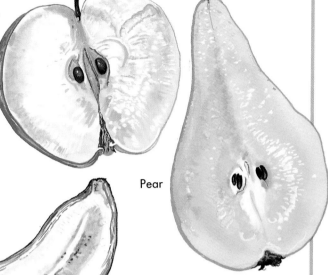

Apple

Pear

Banana

Growing Wild Trees

Try growing some wild seeds and fruits, such as acorns, conkers, elderberries, hawthorns and hazelnut which are easy to find. Make up, or buy, a tray of potting compost. Make rows in the compost about 1 centimetre deep with the end of a pencil. Sprinkle about 50 of the smaller seeds along these rows. Make holes 2 centimetres deep for the medium-sized berries, and 4 centimetres deep for the large seeds and cover them with soil. Put them in a warm sunny position and keep the compost moist. Do not be disappointed if they don't germinate. Some seeds lie **dormant** for many years.

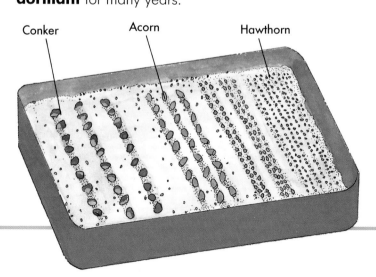

Conker

Acorn

Hawthorn

Walking Seeds

Plants cannot walk. Trees and other plants make tasty fruits round their seeds in order to tempt animals to eat them. In this way the seeds can be carried all over the world inside an animal's gut. The fleshy part is digested, but the hard case around the seed will be left in the animal's dropping.

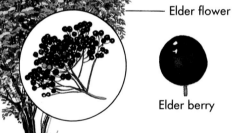

Elder flower

Elder berry

Elder tree

Estimating Elder Seeds

Count how many seeds there are in one elderberry by squashing it. Count how many berries there are in the cluster. Estimate how many clusters of berries are on the tree. You can now estimate how many seeds there are altogether.

How Do Other Trees Travel?

Animals such as squirrels store nuts and often forget where they have put them, and these later grow into trees. In autumn when there is plenty of wild food about, badgers and foxes will often eat fruits and berries as an alternative to meat. The pips and seeds will be discarded in their droppings. These may grow into new trees a long way from the parent tree and this is called dispersal.

Squirrel storing nuts

Barometer Cones

Collect some cones from different **conifers**. Larch, pine or spruce are good. Put some in a dry, warm place (like the airing cupboard) and others in a damp place. Leave them for several days and see what happens. Cones have moisture sensitive cells at their centre. These cause the folds of the cone to open when the weather is dry and close when it is damp.

Catkins and Pods

Birch seeds hang down from the tree, tucked in the folds of a catkin. When the seeds are ripe, the folds of the catkin open and the wind blows them out. Laburnum, locust and Judas trees produce seeds in pods. On a very hot dry day the pods burst open. They twist, causing the seeds to be thrown out in different directions.
Warning: laburnum seeds are very poisonous.

Crossbills

Crossbills are the only birds that can extract the seeds from a closed cone. This means that there is always plenty of food for them to eat. A nest of young crossbills can eat over 85,000 pine seeds as they grow up. The parents twist the cones off the stem then prise open the cones using their specially designed beak. Try extracting a seed using a pair of tweezers.

Cone closed in damp weather

Cones open in dry weather

Birch seeds

Laburnum pod bursts open

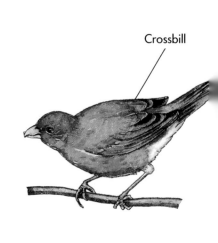

Crossbill

Flying Seeds Game

Equipment: paper, paint, glue.

Make a tree and base as shown. Make 20 seeds out of small rectangles of paper: twist them in the middle. Balance the seeds in the tree. To play the game, blow gently on your tree. If your seed lands in the flower bed or on the lawn it will be picked up by a careful gardener (remove these ones). Seeds landing on concrete or in the pond will not germinate. If the seed lands in the wild garden, it can germinate. To find out if it germinates you must throw the dice:

- If you throw a 1, your seedling is killed by weedkiller.
- Throw a 2, seedling killed by drought.
- Throw a 3, weather is warm, wet and sunny. Seedling survives.
- Throw a 4, frosts kill your seedling.
- Throw a 5, seedling is cared for and watered by a child. It survives.
- Throw a 6, squirrel eats seedling.

Play the game five times (100 seeds in total). How many grow into new trees?

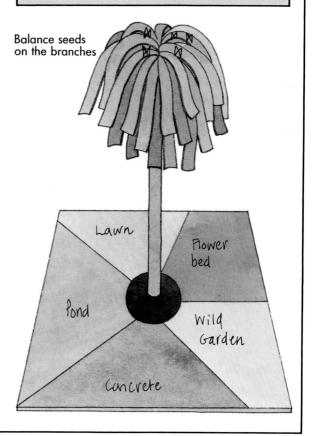

Balance seeds on the branches

Lawn

Flower bed

Pond

Wild Garden

Concrete

Helicopter Seeds

Some seeds, such as lime are formed so that as they drop they start to spin like the blades of a helicopter.

Make your own lime 'helicopter' by cutting a shape like this in thin card. Cut along the dotted lines. Stick a small blob of Blu-tack on the bottom. This provides the weight of the seed. Fold the 'blades' of the helicopter up at point (A) and down at point (B). You may need to experiment with the angle to get your seed to fly properly.

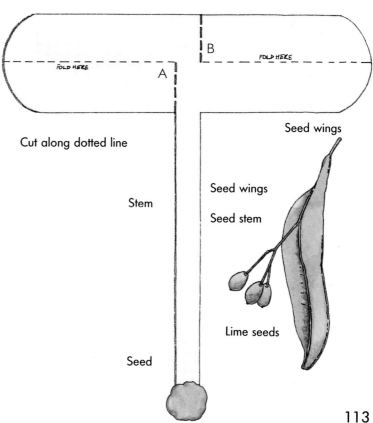

B

FOLD HERE

A

FOLD HERE

Cut along dotted line

Stem

Seed

Seed wings

Seed wings

Seed stem

Lime seeds

Where Seeds Come From

If you look at some trees you can see the seeds developing at different stages from the ovary of the flower to the fully grown fruit or seed.

Look at sycamore, cherry, elder and apple trees when they are flowering and notice the tiny fruits beginning to grow where the petals have fallen off. A good way to watch the growth of a flower into a seed is to tie a bright piece of wool round the stem of the flower so you always know which one to look at. Return ever few days to see what has happened. Remember not all ova are fertilized and grow into seeds.

Stigma   Style

Anther

Stamen

Petal

Sepal

Ovary

Ovule

Cherry flower

Growing fruit

Male and Female

Look closely into some flowers on a tree. Look for the **stamens** with **pollen** (the male part) and the **ovary** (the female part). This picture shows you what they look like. Pollen from one flower must be transferred to the ovary of another flower, then it can grow into a fruit or seed.

Be a 'Feather Bee'

You can help to make fruit trees grow more fruit by pollinating the flowers: using a feather or your finger pick up pollen from one flower and then dust it onto another flower. This takes the male pollen to the female part. They grow together to make a seed. Fruit-growers spray their trees with insecticides. It is important that this does not harm the bees. They fly to the flower looking for nectar (food). They also collect pollen to feed their young. Some of this pollen is brushed off onto other flowers.

This photograph shows a bee collecting nectar and pollen on fruit flowers.

114

Cooking with Fruits

Wash eight elderberry clusters and remove the berries. Core and slice four apples and one orange with its peel on. Simmer all the fruit for half an hour. If necessary, add sugar. Transfer to an oven-proof dish, make a pastry top and cook for half an hour at 180°C until lightly brown.

A pleasant summer drink can be made from elderflowers. Pick 15 heads and remove the stalks which taste bitter. Pour in half a litre of boiling water. Add the juice and rind of two lemons and a 100 grams of sugar. Strain and serve. Use other fruits also.

Fruit Printing

Moist, firm fruits are good to use as 'printing blocks'. Apples, strawberries, and pears work well. Mix up some paints in flat containers. Cut the fruit in half and dip it into the paint. Press the fruit gently onto a clean piece of paper and lift.

Help a Hazel

In some trees the male and female parts are separate. The hazel tree has small red flowers. Look for them in this picture. The male pollen is produced on catkins that hang down from the branches. The flowers are so small that insects like the bee do not bother to visit them. You can 'help a hazel' by taking pollen from the catkins to the flower. You imitate the wind by gently shaking the twig. If the pollen is ripe, it falls easily. Willow, poplar, birch, alder and oak also have hanging catkins carrying the male pollen. They all need the wind to help them pollinate the female flowers.

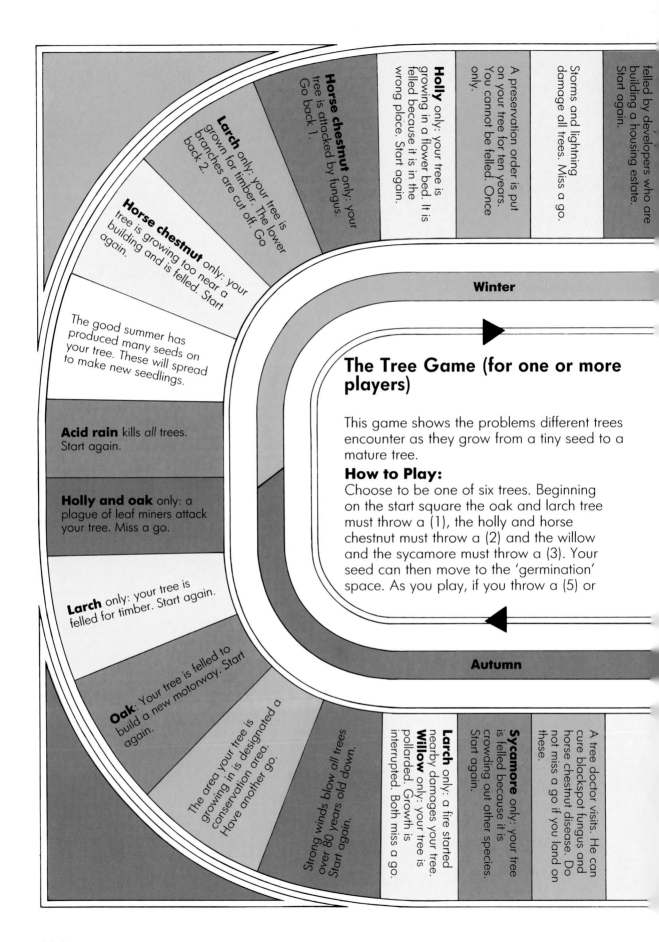

Winter

The Tree Game (for one or more players)

This game shows the problems different trees encounter as they grow from a tiny seed to a mature tree.

How to Play:

Choose to be one of six trees. Beginning on the start square the oak and larch tree must throw a (1), the holly and horse chestnut must throw a (2) and the willow and the sycamore must throw a (3). Your seed can then move to the 'germination' space. As you play, if you throw a (5) or

Autumn

felled by developers who are building a housing estate. Start again.

Storms and lightning damage all trees. Miss a go.

A preservation order is put on your tree for ten years. You cannot be felled. Once only.

Holly only: your tree is growing in a flower bed. It is felled because it is in the wrong place. Start again.

Horse chestnut only: your tree is attacked by fungus. Go back 1.

Larch only: your tree is grown for timber. The lower branches are cut off. Go back 2.

Horse chestnut only: your tree is growing too near a building and is felled. Start again.

The good summer has produced many seeds on your tree. These will spread to make new seedlings.

Acid rain kills *all* trees. Start again.

Holly and oak only: a plague of leaf miners attack your tree. Miss a go.

Larch only: your tree is felled for timber. Start again.

Oak: Your tree is felled to build a new motorway. Start again.

The area your tree is growing in is designated a conservation area. Have another go.

Strong winds blow all trees over 80 years old down. Start again.

Larch only: a fire started nearby damages your tree. **Willow** only: your tree is pollarded. Growth is interrupted. Both miss a go.

Sycamore only: your tree is felled because it is crowding out other species. Start again.

A tree doctor visits. He can cure blackspot fungus and horse chestnut disease. Do not miss a go if you land on these.

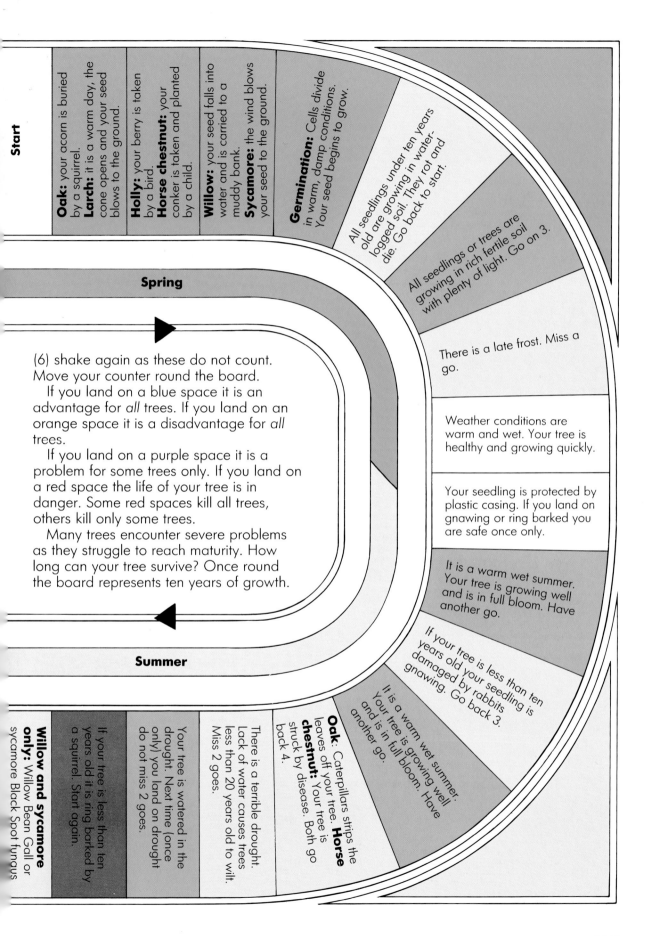

Start

Oak: your acorn is buried by a squirrel.
Larch: it is a warm day, the cone opens and your seed blows to the ground.
Holly: your berry is taken by a bird.
Horse chestnut: your conker is taken and planted by a child.
Willow: your seed falls into water and is carried to a muddy bank.
Sycamore: the wind blows your seed to the ground.

Germination: Cells divide in warm, damp conditions. Your seed begins to grow.

All seedlings under ten years old are growing in water-logged soil. They rot and die. Go back to start.

All seedlings or trees are growing in rich fertile soil with plenty of light. Go on 3.

There is a late frost. Miss a go.

Weather conditions are warm and wet. Your tree is healthy and growing quickly.

Your seedling is protected by plastic casing. If you land on gnawing or ring barked you are safe once only.

It is a warm wet summer. Your tree is growing well and is in full bloom. Have another go.

If your tree is less than ten years old your seedling is damaged by rabbits gnawing. Go back 3.

It is a warm wet summer. Your tree is growing well and is in full bloom. Have another go.

Oak: Caterpillars strips the leaves off your tree. **Horse chestnut:** Your tree is struck by disease. Both go back 4.

There is a terrible drought. Lack of water causes trees less than 20 years old to wilt. Miss 2 goes.

Your tree is watered in the drought. Next time (once only) you land on drought do not miss 2 goes.

Willow and sycamore only: If your tree is less than ten years old it is ring barked by a squirrel. Start again.

Willow and sycamore only: Willow Bean Gall or sycamore Black Spot fungus

Spring

Summer

(6) shake again as these do not count. Move your counter round the board.

If you land on a blue space it is an advantage for *all* trees. If you land on an orange space it is a disadvantage for *all* trees.

If you land on a purple space it is a problem for *some* trees only. If you land on a red space the life of your tree is in danger. Some red spaces kill all trees, others kill only some trees.

Many trees encounter severe problems as they struggle to reach maturity. How long can your tree survive? Once round the board represents ten years of growth.

The World of a Tree

Every tree is a world of its own. It is home for thousands of different plants and creatures. We have found over 100 different species of animal and plant living in or using our oak. Up to 250 species of insect like living on oak trees.

Creatures and plants are **dependent** on each other in different ways. Many mammals, birds and insects are dependent on trees and plants as a source of food and shelter. Some creatures and trees are mutually dependent: they both need each other to survive. For example, this tree provides food for minibeasts and small mammals, and they help to convert the tree's decaying leaves into rich soil.

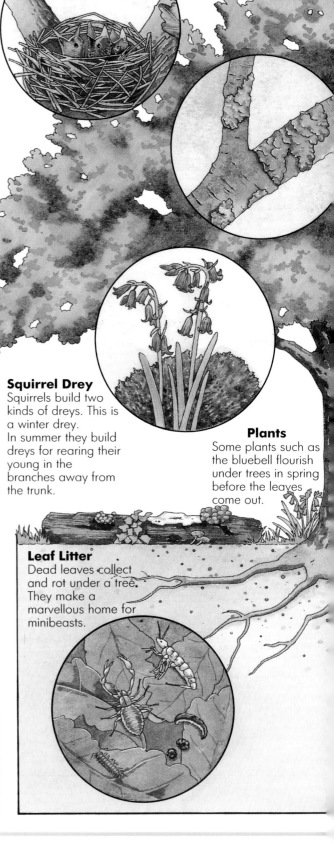

Squirrel Drey
Squirrels build two kinds of dreys. This is a winter drey. In summer they build dreys for rearing their young in the branches away from the trunk.

Plants
Some plants such as the bluebell flourish under trees in spring before the leaves come out.

Leaf Litter
Dead leaves collect and rot under a tree. They make a marvellous home for minibeasts.

▼ Spotted Woodpecker

Nests
Small birds nest in small trees. Larger birds nest in high open branches.

Other Things to Look For

Some things are harmful to trees. Ivy can grow as high as the tree itself. This weakens the tree by reducing the light supply to the leaves and prevents them photosynthesising. Fungi grow on both dead and living trees. Bracket fungi are known to kill many trees every year.

Some insects are harmful to trees. The elm bark beetle has caused the death of millions of trees in Europe. The beetle carries a fungus that kills the tree. You may notice some of the leaves on your tree have pale wiggly lines or blotches on them. These are the secret passages made by leaf-mining grubs which tunnel, eating between the different layers of a leaf and later turn into moths. Another word for a tree's community is its **ecosystem.**

Algae and Lichens
Algae are minute single-cell plants that often grow on tree trunks. They look like a fine green powder. Lichens can be green, grey, yellow or orange.

Fox Home
Foxes often dig their dens among the roots of trees where they can rear up to five young cubs every year.

Deer Browsing
Deer and cattle often eat leaves off the lower branches of trees. In autumn deer will also eat acorns and beech mast.

Who Lives in Your Tree?

You can find out who lives in your tree by shaking the branches and catching the creatures as they fall out. Get two friends to hold a white sheet out under the branch while you shake. Try using stiff white paper if you have no-one to help you.

The Blue Carpet

In spring, under the trees in some woods, the ground looks blue. Bluebells thrive by growing in spring when there are few leaves on the trees and plenty of light can filter through. Plants need light to survive and grow. Can anything grow under a tree in summer when there is a dense covering of leaves? Check what grows at different times of the year.

Cotton sheet

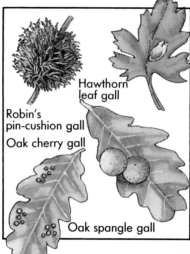

Robin's pin-cushion gall

Hawthorn leaf gall

Oak cherry gall

Oak spangle gall

Plant galls are abnormal swellings on the leaves of plants. They are the result of attack by fungi or insects, mites or even small worms. The largest are caused by insects which lay their eggs in the tissue of the leaf. When the larvae grow up they cause huge swelling of the leaf.

Looking in Leaf Litter

When dead leaves collect under a tree, they form what is known as **leaf litter**. Find out what lives in the leaf litter or soil beneath your tree. Here are some of the creatures you might find. They help to decompose the leaves and twigs that fall off your tree. Collect some in a tub and see how they behave.

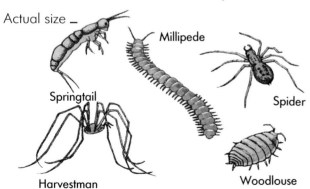

Actual size —

Springtail

Millipede

Spider

Harvestman

Woodlouse

▼ A carpet of bluebells.

Mammal Signs

It is difficult to see wild animals in their natural habitat (home). This is because they are wary of humans, and because many are nocturnal. Even if we can't see animals such as foxes, badgers, hedgehogs and rabbits, there are often plenty of clues to look for. Footprints tell us which animals are about, where they came from and where they went to. Droppings tell us what the animal ate during a recent meal.

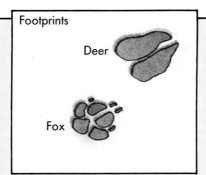

Footprints

Deer

Fox

Food remains

Hazelnut split by squirrel

Hazelnut eaten by mouse

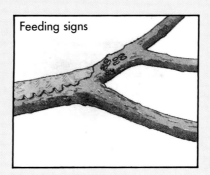

Feeding signs

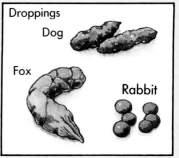

Droppings

Dog

Fox

Rabbit

Bird Signs

Look for feathers, droppings and pellets to see which birds visit the tree. A pile of droppings all in one place usually means a bird has been roosting there. Look for the short downy 'body' feathers and the longer wing and tail feathers. Owl pellets are a mass of fur and bones that the owl cannot digest. They are coughed up again as a pellet.

More Plants on Trees

Look for mosses growing on and under your tree. Make a miniature moss garden where tiny creatures might like to live, using small flowers and stones. Mistletoe is a **parasite** (something that lives and feeds off another living thing). Birds wipe the seeds from their beaks onto the tree. Roots then grow into the wood and suck up the **sap**.

Fluffy down feathers

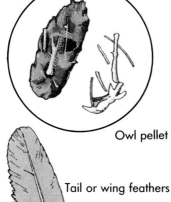

Owl pellet

Tail or wing feathers

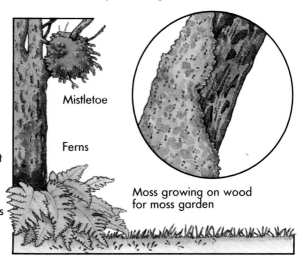

Mistletoe

Ferns

Moss growing on wood for moss garden

The Importance of Wood

Wood has been used by humans for thousands of years. It was first fashioned into simple tools and burned to produce heat. Wood has been used to build houses, bridges, ships and furniture. Wood is used to make paper so without trees the printing revolution could never have taken place.

▲ Wood is used for many purposes. Many of the objects in this picture are made of wood.

A World Without Wood

How many things can you find in the photograph on this page that are made of wood? There are a great many if you look closely enough. Now try noting down all the things in your house that are made of wood. You will find that a great many things in your house rely on wood for their basic structure or support.

A World Without Trees

Every time you switch on a light, energy is being used. That energy originally came from trees and is now in its turn causing the death of other trees. Much of the electricity we use today is generated by burning coal (made from dead plants and trees). When coal is burnt, acid gases are released and collect high up in the atmosphere. Here they mix with water to form **acid rain**. Acid rain has terrible effects on the environment. It pollutes rivers and lakes, killing fish and plants; it eats into stone and destroys the surface of buildings; it helps to poison the soil and damages trees eventually killing them. About 15 per cent of forests in Europe have been destroyed already. Acid rain can be as strong as vinegar.

Cars of the Future

Cars are also big polluters. They give off huge amounts of pollutant gases. Cars have been developed with special devices to make exhaust gases harmless. The Brazilians have come up with an interesting alternative: they run cars on alcohol made from sugar cane, which, if successful, will save much of the Earth's resources.

Acid rain damage

Car exhaust causes acid rain

Making Paper from Paper

Equipment: Newspaper, garden netting, bucket, saucepan, old blanket.

To make your own paper, wash a large newspaper. Tear (or use a liquidiser) it into shreds, put it into a bucket and pour in hot water. Allow to soak overnight. Boil this mixture in a large old saucepan until the paper has dissolved into a mushy stew. Let it stand and cool so that there is an even layer floating near the surface. Dip the netting into the pan and lift it out flat so that the pulp makes a layer of even thickness. Let the water drain away, then turn the paper out onto a piece of old blanket. Add a few layers so that the paper will hold together. Place another piece of old blanket on top and then a wooden board. Tread on the board to squeeze out all the water. Lift the blanket off, and leave to dry.

Did you know? Big paper mills can make over 30 kilometres of paper per hour working day and night. That is 720 kilometres a day!

Plenty of Paper

Paper is important as a way of recording and passing on information. We use it for newspapers, books, maps, letters and many other forms of writing. Paper can also be used for other things: tissues, paper towels, bags and packets. Look around your house, you will find many different uses for paper.

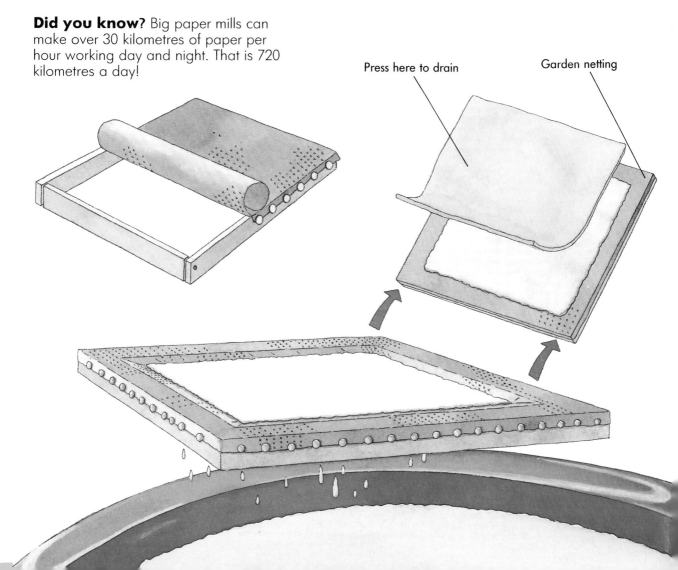

Press here to drain

Garden netting

Using Wood

It is very important that the woods that now survive do so for many years to come. Woods survive best if they are properly looked after and one way of helping is making sure that the trees are not overcrowded. Cutting some down actually helps the others to grow better and provides valuable wood for building and heating, and paper-making.

Managing Woodland

People look after woodland to make it grow the way they want it to. Hazel trees are coppiced: they are cut back to ground level to allow new straight stems to grow up. These are used as poles or for fencing. Willow trees are pollarded: the branches are cut back at a higher level and the willow 'wands' are harvested for basket weaving.

Coppiced at ground level

Pollarded at 3–4 metres

Making a Garden Broom

Peg

Twigs bound with string

Finished broom

Get an adult to help you make this. Cut a 1 metre length of ash, lime or hazel wood to use as the handle. Use birch twigs for the head. Drill a 2 centimetre hole through the handle. Fit a peg tightly into this hole. Hold a bundle of twigs around the handle and bind them tightly, then fasten the cord carefully to the peg. These brooms are excellent for sweeping up autumn leaves.

Equipment: Wooden pole, birch twigs, cord.

Wood Sculpture: Trees sometimes appear in the most extraordinary shapes if they have to grow around an obstacle. You may find a particularly interesting piece of wood you want to keep as a natural sculpture.

Building a Bird Box

You will need a plank of wood about 150mm wide, 15 millimetres thick and 1.5 metres long. Mark on the measurements of each part before beginning to cut your wood. Saw up the six pieces and sand the edges smooth. Drill a hole about 27mm in diameter in the front of your box. If you make the hole a little larger (up to 32mm) you will attract different kinds of bird to nest there. Assemble your box by joining it together as shown. Use screws or galvanised nails. Fasten the lid with a catch to stop cats interfering.

Equipment: Plank of wood, drill, screws.

Size of Hole

Make sure the size of the hole is the same as shown here. The box is designed only for quite small birds and if the hole is too big they will be forced out by stronger species.

You can attract different types of bird by making a more open box. Saw off the upper half of the front by sawing along the dotted lines as shown.

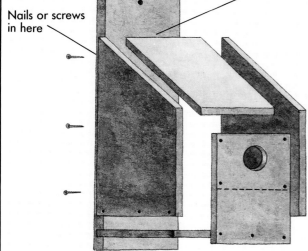

Nails or screws in here

Hinge lid with rubber

Side 200mm

Side 250mm

Roof 200mm

Base 110mm

Front 200mm

Back 450mm

Where to Put It

Hang or nail your box to a tree about 3–5 metres off the ground and safely out of reach of any cats. Do not let it face into strong sunlight as this can kill nestlings. Facing north-east or south-east is preferable. Remember to clean the box every autumn so that old nest material doesn't collect inside. If you do not the box will become clogged up and new birds will not come and nest inside.

Remember to hang the box out of reach of any cats.

Remember to hang your box in the shade.

Disappearing Forests

Many thousands of years ago three-quarters of all land was covered by trees. Through disease, fire and felling between 70 and 90 per cent has been destroyed. Some countries still have large areas of rain forest but these are rapidly being destroyed.

The Rich Rain Forest and How It Helps us

Rain forests are full of plants and animals, many of which are useful to us. Some 40 per cent of medical chemicals in the United States come from rain forests. Many more chemicals are still undiscovered. Trees also produce a large amount of the oxygen that we breathe. This picture shows that leaves take in carbon dioxide (CO_2) that we breathe out, and give off oxygen (O_2). Imagine what would happen if all the trees and plants that make oxygen for us were destroyed. Every minute over 100 acres of forest are destroyed. Once the trees are gone the rich soil is washed away by heavy rains so no more trees can grow.

▲ Rain forests are cut down to provide grazing land and places for people to live. Often these ventures fail but the forest is terminally damaged.

How You Can Help

We need wood, and it is not a bad thing to fell trees so long as they are replanted. You can help by planting trees in your garden or at school. You can often find self-sown tree seedlings near a well established tree that might not survive well in the shade. These could be moved to a more suitable open place. You can, of course, buy trees at a tree nursery.

You can help by recycling old newspaper. Some councils now have special collecting points. Find out by phoning your local council offices. Trees are destroyed by acid rain. Help prevent this by saving energy and recycling.

Many South American Indians live in the rain forest. They have a legend that tells how the trees hold up the sky and that if they are cut down a great catastrophe will come about.

Did you know? It takes one tree to make 250 disposable nappies. Can you estimate how many trees each baby needs in a year? Every minute an area of rain forest the size of 20 football pitches is destroyed.

Acid Rain

Trees and Leaves Quiz

True or False?

1. Trees cannot make their own food. All food enters through the roots.

2. All trees drop their leaves in Autumn.

True or False?

True or False?

3. Tree flowers can be pollinated by insects and wind.

SUN

CO_2

O_2

4. Buds always have flowers in them.

5. What's wrong with this picture?

True or False?

Answers

1. *False. Trees make food by photosynthesis in their leaves. They do absorb water and minerals and other substances through their roots.*

2. *False. Deciduous trees drop their leaves in Autumn. Evergreens shed their leaves gradually throughout the year.*

3. *True. Wind transports the pollen from the hazel catkin to the flower. Many trees, such as the cherry tree, are pollinated by insects.*

4. *False. Not all buds contain flowers. Many contain leaves instead.*

5. *Leaves absorb CO_2 (carbon dioxide) and give off O_2 (oxygen). Flowers would not be able to develop under the branches of such a large tree, there would be not be enough light.*

THE SEASONS

This section will help you learn about seasons. Think about the seasons as the weather and temperature changes throughout the year.

There are four main sections in this book:

- Spring
- Summer
- Autumn
- Winter

Use the symbols below to help you identify the three kinds of practical activities in this book.

EXPERIMENTS

TRICKS

THINGS TO MAKE

Introduction

As our planet Earth circles around the Sun each year, the weather changes in a seasonal pattern. During the warm months of Summer, more sunlight energy reaches the surface of the Earth than in the cold Winter months. The closer you live to the North (or South) Pole the more pronounced this change is. Many plants and animals have a way of life that follows this yearly pattern of the seasons.

In this section you will find experiments to help you discover for yourself how living things adapt to the changing seasons. The first two pages in each section look at the weather typical of the season. Following that, you will find experiments exploring the way in which animals and plants respond to the season. Concluding each section you will find activities that use natural materials of the season.

The seasons are not clear cut like days or months. For example, there are often warm weeks in the middle of Winter. In some years, Summer takes a long time to arrive. Because of this you will find that many of the experiments from one season may be done at other times of the year.

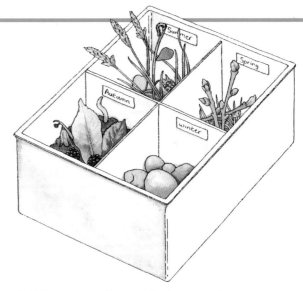

▲ What is weather and what are the seasons? (pages 132 and 133)

▲ What happens to trees as the seasons pass? (pages 137, 145, 153, and 161)

▼ How can you record and forecast the weather? (pages 132, 133, 143, and 151)

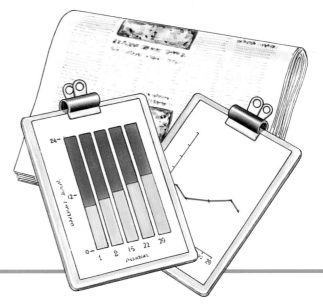

▼ How do plants survive the seasons? (pages 136, 144, 145, 152, and 153)

▲ What happens to plants in extreme conditions? (pages 136 and 152)

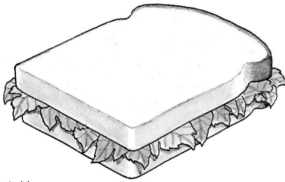

▲ How can you make seasonal snacks for birds? (pages 139, 141, and 163) and people? (pages 148, 149, and 163)

▲ How can you capture the colours of the seasons? (pages 137, 140, 143, 148, and 149)

▼ Taking a lesson from nature. How can you recycle your rubbish? (pages 160 and 163)

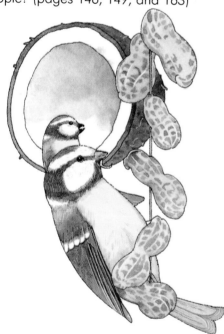

▲ Animals survive the seasons: How do animals find food and stay warm? (pages 134, 135, 138, and 139)

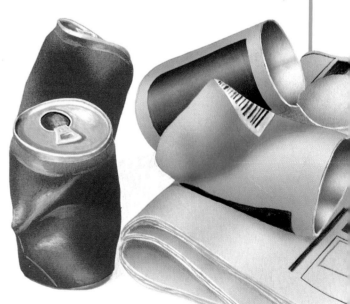

What Season is it?

Look around outside. What season is it? Sometimes it is easy to decide. You will be able to make up your mind by looking at the weather and what is happening in the natural world. However, you may have a problem deciding which season it is. To help you, these two pages contain information about the weather and the seasons.

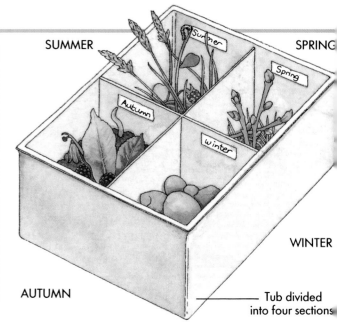

SUMMER   SPRING

WINTER

AUTUMN   Tub divided into four sections

The Four Season Box

To help you decide which season it is, make a four season box. Divide a plastic tub into four sections as shown, using card and sticky tape. Label the sections Spring, Summer, Autumn and Winter. Now look around outside for things that make you think of any one of the seasons, and put them in that section of the box. For example, a fallen leaf might remind you of Autumn, or a flower petal of Spring. If you see something that is too big to go in the box (perhaps somebody in a woolly hat makes you think of Winter), write it down on a piece of paper to put in the box. The section that fills up fastest will probably be the season that you are in at the moment.

▶ You can make up a picture of the season like this. Stick pieces of double-sided sticky tape on a small piece of card. Carry this around with you and collect anything that indicates to you the season that you are in.

Double-sided sticky tape

The Spirit of the Season

Each season has a different 'feel'. To capture the spirit of the season go to your favourite outdoors place, or sit by an open window with a sheet of paper and a pencil. Make yourself comfortable then close your eyes and listen. Now look around. How do your surroundings feel and smell? Write down words as they come to mind. Now cut the words up and arrange them to make sense, adding joining words if necessary. Your 'poem' will capture the spirit of the season.

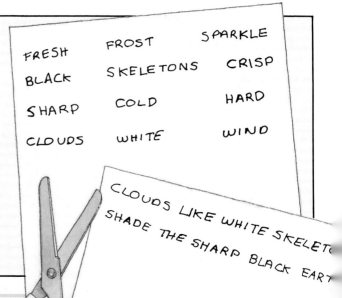

FRESH   FROST   SPARKLE

BLACK   SKELETONS   CRISP

SHARP   COLD   HARD

CLOUDS   WHITE   WIND

CLOUDS LIKE WHITE SKELETO

SHADE THE SHARP BLACK EART

Windy Weather

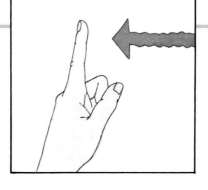

The strength of the wind, and where it blows from, will affect the weather. Wind blowing in from the sea may bring rain. Wind from the south might bring hot weather. Here is an easy way to find out which way the wind is blowing from. Lick the pad of one finger and hold it above your head. When the finger is facing the wind it will feel cool. Use a compass, or ask someone, to find out which direction this is. Use these pictures showing the Beaufort Scale of wind speeds to work out how strong the wind is.

Nature's Forecasters

The seasons and the weather affect plants and animals. For centuries people have used these reactions to forecast the weather. For example, the mistle thrush is known as the 'storm cock' because it often sings from a tree-top in windy weather. The arrival of the swallows means that summer is on the way—but one swallow does not make a summer! Here are some other sayings that have developed from observing plants and animals:

'When the swallows fly high, it will be dry.'
'If the cows are lying down it will rain.'
'A good Autumn for fruit means a hard Winter to come.'

See if you can find some more weather sayings, and test them to see if they are true.

Swallow

Thrush

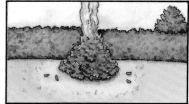

Force 0 Calm: leaves don't even stir.

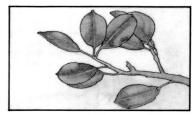

Force 1–3 Light breeze: leaves and twigs start to move.

Force 4–5 Moderate wind: small trees start to sway.

Force 6–7 Strong wind: big trees sway.

Force 8–9 Gale: branches blown off.

Force 10–12 Storm and hurricane: trees are blown over.

Winter

In the north, Winter is a cold time of short days and long nights. For many animals and plants life is hard. They must survive until the warmer weather arrives. Their survival will depend on how well prepared they are, and how severe the Winter is. Find out in this section what weather is in store for them, and how they will survive it.

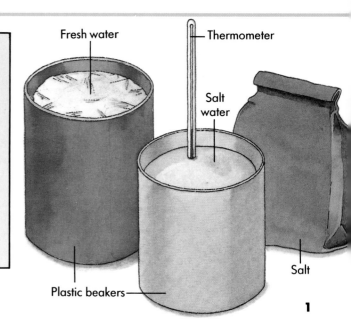

Fresh water
Thermometer
Salt water
Salt
Plastic beakers

1

Freezing Water

1. When the temperature falls below 0° Celsius water freezes from a liquid into a solid. Put a plastic cup of water into the freezer. Check the temperature of the water at intervals to see at what temperature the ice starts to form. Repeat the experiment, but add salt to the water first. Salty water, such as the sea, stays liquid even below 0° Celsius.

2. Fill a container with fresh snow. Level off the snow, but don't press it down. Leave the snow to melt, then look to see how much water is left. Snow takes up more space than water, chiefly because it contains a lot of air. The space between the top of the melted water and the top of the container shows you roughly how much air there was in the snow.

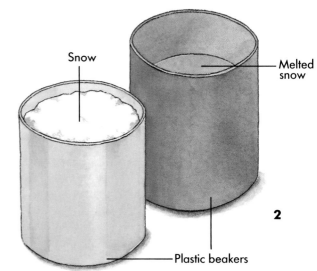

Snow
Melted snow
Plastic beakers

2

Life under the Snow

Because snow contains so much air, it is a good insulator. This means that it acts like a blanket and helps warm things to stay warm! The snow also helps to protect plants from damage by the cold winds and frosts. For animals that cannot bury themselves under the snow life is more difficult. Deer cannot find plants to eat; owls and stoats must search for the small mammals they need to eat for energy. To stop using up valuable energy, some animals hibernate in the Winter.

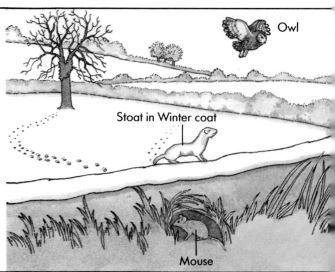

Owl
Stoat in Winter coat
Mouse

Life under the Ice

In the experiment opposite you will observe that as ice starts to form it floats on top of the water. A layer of ice on a pond has the same effect as a layer of snow on the ground; it helps to insulate the water underneath, so that it takes longer for the rest of the water to freeze. Plants under the ice layer are not damaged, and fish can also survive. However, this is no help to ducks. They cannot reach the water and have to migrate elsewhere.

▲ Water in the air condenses as the temperature falls. In cold weather the water forms crystals of ice and often appears as white 'hoar frost'. Each crystal has perfect six-sided symmetry like a snowflake.

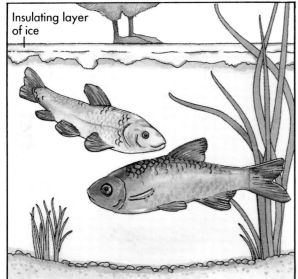

Insulating layer of ice

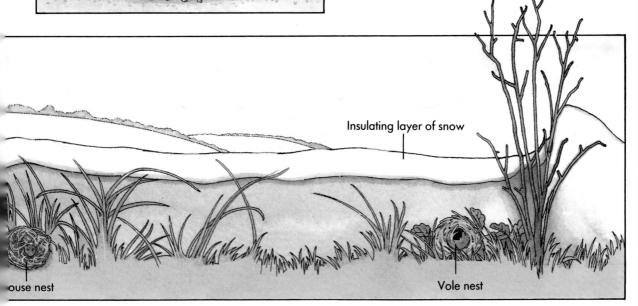

Insulating layer of snow

ouse nest

Vole nest

A Winter Wander

Many plants die back in the Winter because they are too delicate to survive the frost. However, some are well suited to the harsh conditions, and will even flower. Take a walk on a warm Winter's day and see if any flowers are out. Look to see if they are in the sun or in the shade. Plants that flower in cold temperatures often have tough and waxy leaves to stop them drying out.

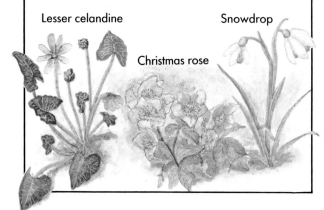

Lesser celandine

Snowdrop

Christmas rose

Trees in Winter

A tree needs to make food to stay alive. The food is made in the leaves, using sunlight energy to make sugars by a process called **photosynthesis** . At the same time water is lost from the leaves, and the tree must replace this water by absorbing fresh water from the soil into its roots. During the Winter less sunlight is available to make food. At the same time the water in the soil becomes frozen, so it cannot be absorbed. If a tree kept losing water

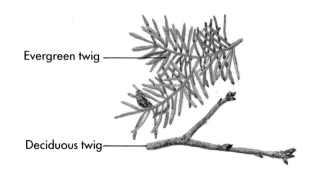

Evergreen twig ——

Deciduous twig ——

Plants in the Cold

Do this experiment to find out what happens to plants when the temperature falls below freezing. Put cress seeds on damp tissue paper in two plastic trays. Place container A in a warm cupboard and container B in a freezer. Water the seeds when the paper feels dry and wait to see which seeds grow roots and shoots. Prepare two more trays in the same way, but put both containers in a warm cupboard and leave them to germinate for a few days. Then leave container C in the cupboard, but move D into a freezer. You will be able to watch the effect of the cold on the young seedlings.

A Seeds in warm cupboard

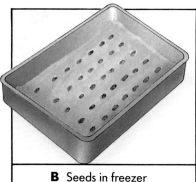

B Seeds in freezer

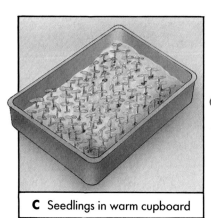

C Seedlings in warm cupboard

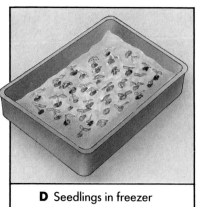

D Seedlings in freezer

through its leaves it would dry out. Look for a **deciduous** twig like the one shown. Deciduous trees lose their leaves in the Winter. The leaves for next year are safe inside the bud. Compare this with a twig from an **evergreen** tree which keeps its leaves in the Winter. The leaves are tough and waxy. They lose only a small amount of water, so the tree can keep them without drying out.

Compare these pictures of a silver birch in Summer and in Winter. Then look at the Winter-time trees shown below. Which of these are deciduous and which are evergreen?

Silver birch in Winter

Silver birch in Summer

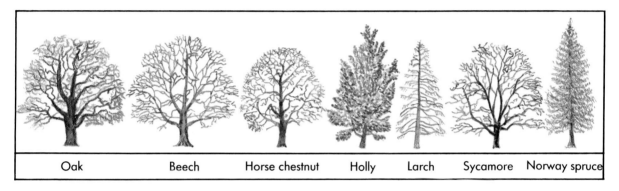

| Oak | Beech | Horse chestnut | Holly | Larch | Sycamore | Norway spruce |

▶ This is an oak tree in Winter. The oak is a deciduous tree: it sheds its leaves for the Winter months. A bare tree like this is sometimes called a tree skeleton. Water is lost through the leaves of a tree by transpiration, so by losing its leaves, the tree saves water. However, without leaves the tree cannot make the food it needs to grow. The tree is dormant in Winter – it stops growing and it needs very little energy to stay alive. To find out what happens to the fallen leaves, see page 161. To find out more about what leaves do, look at page 153.

Keeping Warm

Animals face some of the same problems in Winter as plants do. Water may be difficult to find. Food for energy is in short supply. In addition, warm-blooded creatures must conserve heat. Air is a good insulator and reduces the loss of heat. Humans wear layers of clothing (*see the picture to the right*). Many mammals increase the thickness of their fur, and birds fluff out their feathers to create an insulating layer of air around their bodies. People can turn up the heating in their homes – but animals have to generate their own heat by eating enough of the right foods.

The Survival Game

Mammals require certain things to survive the Winter. For example, they need food, shelter, water and bedding. Write these, and any others you can think of, down on a sheet of paper and cut each word out. Poke a cocktail stick through each one to make a flag. Choose a small area outside and see if you can find all the requirements for survival for one particular animal, for example, a mouse. If you find suitable food (perhaps seeds) mark it with the food flag, and so on. Repeat the game for different animals, and set a time limit. Sometimes you will not be able to find all the requirements. Imagine what would happen to the animal if this happened in real life.

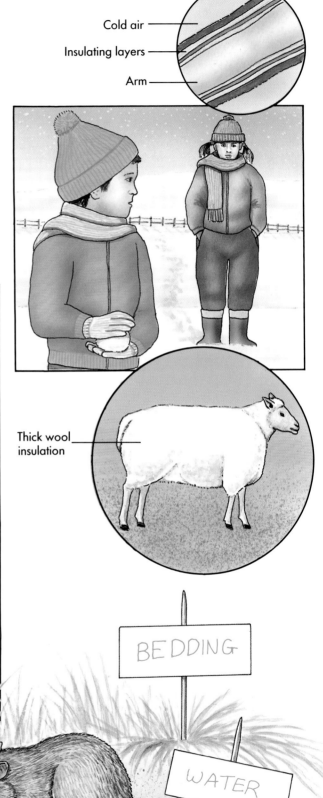

Cold air

Insulating layers

Arm

Thick wool insulation

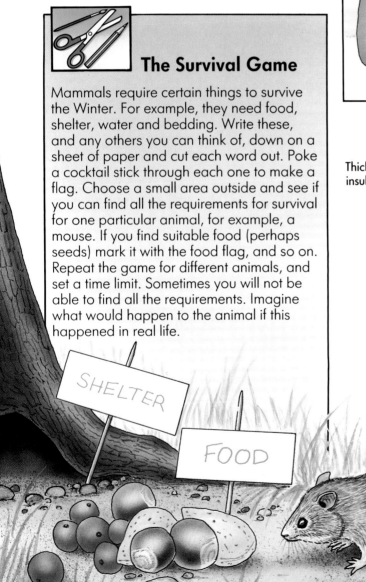

SHELTER

FOOD

BEDDING

WATER

It's a Bird's Life

Like mammals, birds find it hard to find enough food to stay alive in the Winter. You can demonstrate this by collecting natural bird foods outside. Try to fill a matchbox. Do the experiment in different areas, and repeat it in different weather conditions. You can help birds to survive by putting out food, such as seeds, crusts and nuts, and water—away from cats (see page 141). Birds will feed on a wide windowsill. Do not put out mouldy foods, desiccated coconut or very salty foods. Dry food should be soaked first.

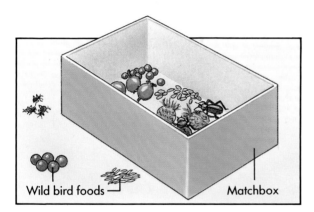

Wild bird foods —   Matchbox

Dozy Minibeasts

The temperature of most mammals and birds is kept constantly high, but the temperature of many other creatures rises and falls with the temperature of their surroundings. When it is cold their temperature drops and they become slow and dozy. This state is called **hibernation**. Hibernating creatures do very little, so they need little energy to stay alive. This means they do not need to eat—they can use stored energy. Look for hibernating minibeasts, but take care not to disturb them or they will waste vital energy. Search under rotten wood and in sheds. Some types of animal change their form completely in the Winter. Adult insects often cannot survive in very cold conditions. Look instead for the egg or the pupa stages of the insect life cycle.

Hungry Owls

Try your luck as a hungry owl in this game. You will need a supply of counters to represent units of energy. At the beginning of the game the owl has a reserve of ten counters stored as fat. Each week she uses up three counters of energy to stay alive. Take these away at the beginning of each round, then throw a dice to find out how many voles the owl catches during the week. For each vole caught, add one counter to the owl. The owl cannot store more than ten units of energy, so if you catch more voles than there is room for, put the extra counters back. Does your owl ever run out of energy, and die? Play the game again in 'Winter conditions'. Many of the voles are now hidden under the snow. Only four voles can be caught each week, so even if you throw a five or six you can add only four counters to the owl. How many weeks does the owl survive?

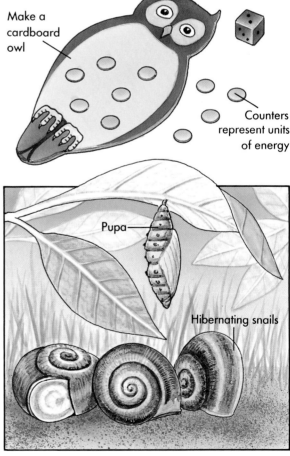

Make a cardboard owl

Counters represent units of energy

Pupa

Hibernating snails

Christmas Decorations

1. Fill a wide-necked bottle with water and rest a hyacinth bulb in the top. The base of the bulb should just touch the top of the water. Keep the bulb somewhere dark while it sprouts. Then bring the plant into the light to allow it to turn green and develop a flower.

2. Stretch two wire clothes' hangers into circles. Lie one on top of the other. Weave long strands of ivy around the circles of wire so that they are bound together. Stick other evergreen branches, such as holly and any other decorations into the circle.

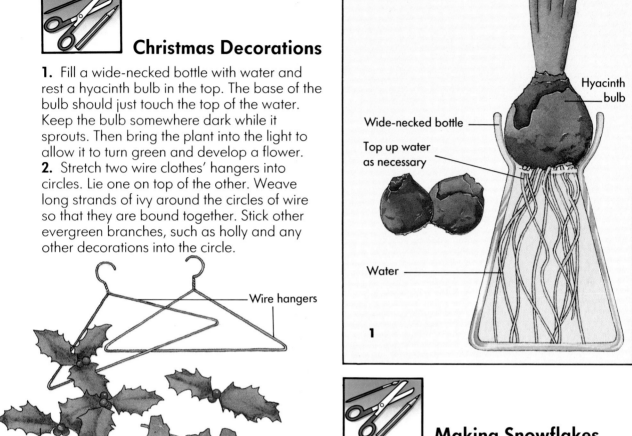

Hyacinth bulb

Wide-necked bottle

Top up water as necessary

Water

1

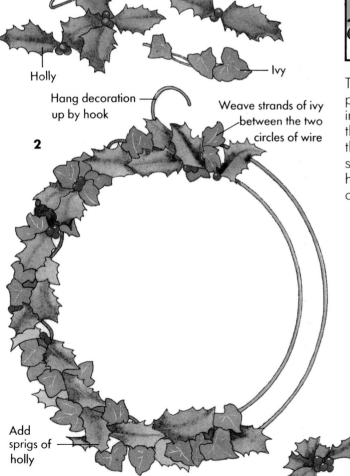

Wire hangers

Holly

Ivy

Hang decoration up by hook

Weave strands of ivy between the two circles of wire

2

Add sprigs of holly

Making Snowflakes

Trace around a plate to make a circle on a piece of paper, and cut it out. Fold the paper in half. The semicircle formed must be folded in thirds, as shown, to form a cone six layers thick. Now cut pieces out along the edges with scissors. When the paper is unfolded you will have a symmetrical snowflake. Snowflakes always have six-sided symmetry.

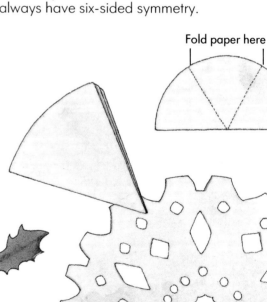

Fold paper here

Feed the Birds

Many animals, including birds, find it difficult to find food during the Winter months. You can help by feeding them (*see page 139*). Making and hanging up a string of monkey nuts will provide you with entertainment, as the more acrobatic birds try to get the nuts out. Ask an adult to help you thread the nuts together with a strong needle.

▼ Even in Winter, preparations are underway for Spring. Take a Winter walk and see if you can see any early flowers, or birds pairing up.

Coconut

Monkey nuts

Make a Plastercast

Mammal and bird footprints in snow soon disappear, but if you find prints in mud you can make a permanent record. Cut a six-centimetre-wide strip of thin card. Make it into a circle just bigger than the print. Tape it firmly, then push it into the ground around the print. Make up some plaster of Paris, stirring until it is creamy. Quickly pour it onto the print, before it becomes solid. Take the cast home when it is hard to touch and remove the card when the plaster is completely hard. If you paint the plaster print you can make animal tracks on paper.

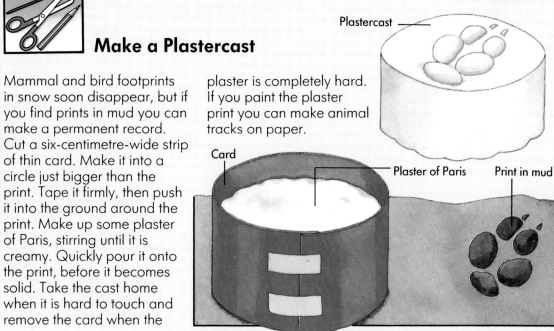

Plastercast

Card

Plaster of Paris

Print in mud

Spring

During the Spring the days quickly become longer. Many plants and animals remain dormant until the increased light and warmth trigger them into action. Often they are waiting for the days to reach a certain length before they stir into activity. Then animals prepare to breed, and plants begin to sprout. The longer days also bring a number of changes in the weather.

Spring Showers

Spring tends to be a showery time of year. Rain is part of the **water cycle**. Water on the surface of the Earth (for example, in the sea or in the soil) turns into vapour, or **evaporates** into the air. To find out why evaporation is faster in the Spring, try this experiment.

Pour the same amount of water into two identical saucers. Place one saucer on a sunny, warm windowsill and the other in the fridge. Look each day to see which evaporates most quickly. More water evaporates in the warm Spring than in the cold Winter. To find out what happens to evaporated water, breathe onto a cold mirror or window. The water in your warm breath condenses as it meets the cold glass.

When warm air containing evaporated water blows over cold land, clouds form and rain falls. This is why Spring tends to be showery.

In the warm

In the fridge

Be a Rain Forecaster

The combination of Spring rain and warm sunshine helps plants to grow. There are a number of signs in nature that are supposed to forecast the coming of rain. You can test some of these old methods to see which work:

A piece of seaweed hung outside becomes wet.
A pine cone closes up.
The scarlet pimpernel flower is known as the 'poor man's weather glass' because it closes up if bad weather is on the way.

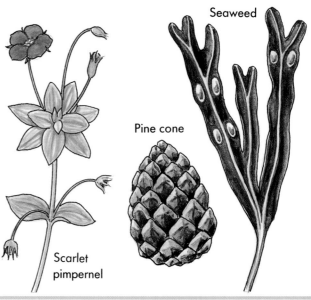

Seaweed

Pine cone

Scarlet pimpernel

The Colour of the Season

Cut out different colours from an old magazine. Take the colours outside and see which of them you can match exactly with the natural things around. Keep the colours that match in a separate box. When you have matched ten colours, look in the box. These are the colours of nature in Spring. You can try this game in different seasons. Spring tends to be a time of light greens. In Autumn you are more likely to find reds and browns.

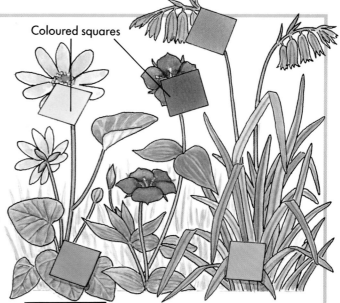

Coloured squares

Longer, Warmer Days

On the same day every week, look up the maximum temperature for your area in a newspaper. Mark it onto a graph for eight weeks and you will see the overall pattern of temperature in Spring. To make your graph, draw two lines on squared paper at right angles. On the bottom line mark the eight dates on which you looked up the temperatures. On the line up the side mark a scale of temperatures 0–30°Celsius.

You can also check how quickly the days lengthen during Spring by making a bar chart. Look up the sunset and sunrise hours in the paper once a week. You can then work out the number of daylight hours in each 24 hours.

The Last Frost

The date of the last frost is important to plants. A late Spring frost will destroy many of the new buds. Some farmers light fires near their fruit trees to stop this happening. To find the date of the last frost put a container of water outside each night. If a layer of ice has formed in the morning, note the date. Even better, leave out an upturned dustbin lid as a bird bath, and check that. Remember to remove the ice to let the birds have their bath!

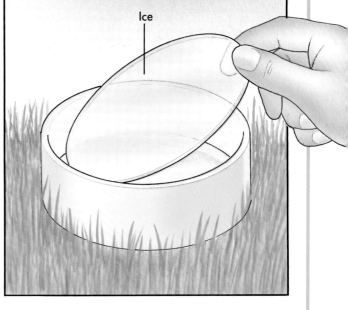

Ice

Hours of daylight

Temperature

A Head Start

Plants must make use of the increasing sunlight energy in the Spring to make food by photosynthesis. The time at which they start to grow is critical. If they start too early they may be killed by frost. If they start too late deciduous trees may have come into leaf overhead, cutting out the vital sunlight energy. Plants growing from seeds will be slow to develop because they have to make all their own food as they grow. However, many plants store food over the Winter. This means that they have a head start in the Spring as they use the stored food to push their way up through the soil. During the rapid growth of the plant much of the stored food energy is used up. This must be replaced later. Some of the food made in the leaves by photosynthesis will be returned to the underground stems. In this way, the cycle can continue again next year.

The food is sometimes stored in bulbs, which are really swollen leaves. Bluebells and ramsons (wild garlic) store their food in this way. In other plants the food is stored in underground stems, for example celandines, violets and primroses. Look in flowerbeds where pets or squirrels have been digging to see which plants have food stored beneath the soil.

Trees in Spring

Deciduous trees in Spring and Winter can be identified by their shape (*see page 137*). It is also possible to identify them by looking at the buds. To identify a twig you will need to answer these questions. What shape are the buds (for example, pointed or round)? What colour are they? Are they in pairs, or do they alternate along the twig?

Mark a twig with some coloured cotton. Look at the buds and write down what you think the tree is. Observe your twig each week until it comes into leaf, when you can identify it by its leaves. How many trees can you identify correctly by looking at the buds?

Ramsons

Bluebell

Primrose

Lesser celandine

Violet

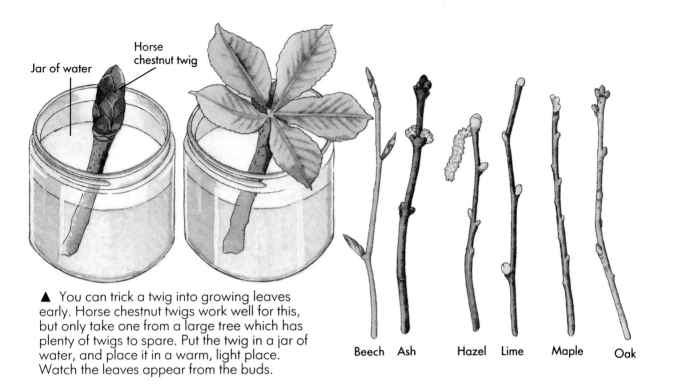

Jar of water

Horse chestnut twig

Beech Ash Hazel Lime Maple Oak

▲ You can trick a twig into growing leaves early. Horse chestnut twigs work well for this, but only take one from a large tree which has plenty of twigs to spare. Put the twig in a jar of water, and place it in a warm, light place. Watch the leaves appear from the buds.

► During the Spring the buds of deciduous trees, such as this oak, open up as the leaves inside grow. Sugars are quickly made in the leaves by photosynthesis, using the stronger sunlight. This process allows the tree to grow. Different trees come into leaf at different times. There is a saying which can be used to predict what the weather is going to be like in the Spring to come. 'If the oak before the ash, we'll have a splash. If the ash before the oak, we'll be soaked'. Watch oak and ash trees as they come into leaf, and see if the saying is true.

Animals in the Spring

As the Spring days become longer, many more animals become active. Animals prepare their homes to be ready for their young when they are born. The migrant birds which have spent the Winter in warmer places return to their breeding grounds to join the resident birds in nest-building. Cold-blooded creatures emerge from their Winter hibernation as their body temperature rises with the surrounding warmth.

When it rains, animals cannot pull on coats and boots as people do. They have other ways of coping. Mammals have grease in their fur, so that the rain runs off instead of soaking in and making the fur soggy. Bird feathers work in a similar way, and birds spend much time preening (oiling their feathers).

Staying dry – mammal

Staying dry – bird

Marking the Boundary

A dog (male) fox marks out the boundaries of his territory by leaving scent. The sense of smell is much less good in humans than in many mammals. Do this experiment to see if you would survive well as a fox. Use a bottle of strong-smelling liquid, such as vinegar or vanilla. Ask a friend to shake a trail of drops across an open space while you are not looking. Now try to find the trail by crawling about, sniffing hard. Mark the point where you find the trail and then start again. Keep marking when you smell the trail and see if you can locate the territory of your 'rival'.

▲ These male oryx are fighting to decide which one will claim a certain territory, and the females within it.

Tree-top Territories

In a single tree, many animals will build a home and rear a family. Often a mammal or bird will hold a **territory**. This is an area which the animal will defend against other animals of the same sort. The territory will be large enough to provide enough food for the new family, and the home or nest will be somewhere in the middle. Some animals, on the other hand, nest together in communities, or colonies.

A male thrush sings from various points in his territory to warn off other thrushes. He will fight off any rivals who come too close. Try making a nest using twigs, leaves, moss and other natural materials as a thrush does. During the Winter months a squirrel makes a drey close to the tree trunk. In the Spring a new one is built farther out in the branches, and this is where the young are born.

Look on wet days for frogs, snails and slugs, and in damp places for woodlice. The problem for these animals in the Summer will not be avoiding the rain, but keeping cool and damp.

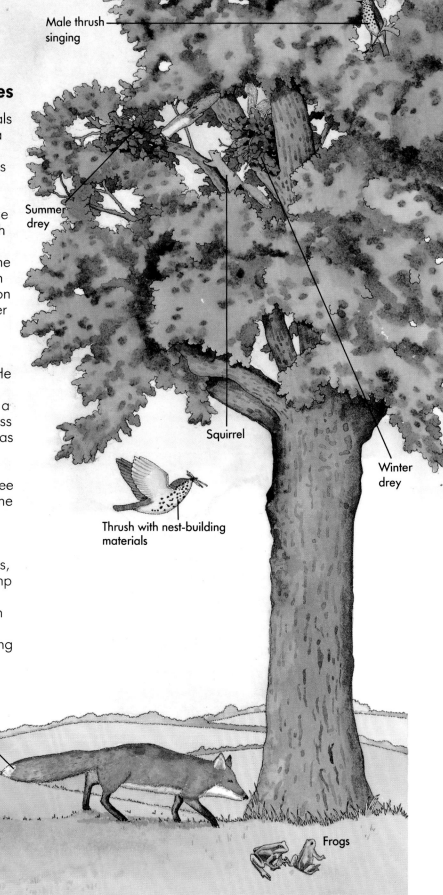

Male thrush singing

Summer drey

Squirrel

Winter drey

Thrush with nest-building materials

Foxes

Frogs

147

Nettle Soup and Hawthorn Nibbles

Equipment: 1 onion—peeled and chopped, 1 potato—peeled and chopped, cooking oil, salt and pepper, yoghurt, stock cube, 20 nettles.

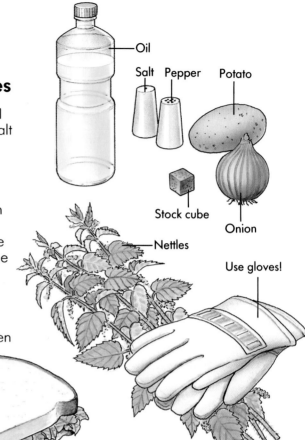

Oil

Salt Pepper Potato

Stock cube

Onion

Nettles

Use gloves!

Collect young nettle shoots from a clean place, wearing rubber gloves. Fry the onion and potato in cooking oil for a few minutes in a saucepan. Chop the leaves off the nettle stalks and add them to the saucepan with the stock cube and one litre of water. Boil until the potato is cooked. Sieve or ask an adult to liquidize the broth, then stir in seasoning and yoghurt if required.

   Young hawthorn leaves make a good addition to salads, and they can also be eaten in a sandwich. They should be washed first.

Hawthorn leaves

Dyeing Naturally

Wool

Birch leaves

Daffodil flowers

The colour of the season can be captured by dyeing wool. To do this you will need an <u>old</u> saucepan (you may not be able to clean it afterwards!). Use either white wool or cotton. Collect one of the plants illustrated, or experiment with other brightly-coloured plants (you could try tree bark, yellow lichens or blackberries). Boil the plant in a little water. When the water is well coloured, cool it and strain the plants off. Now add the white wool and simmer until it has picked up the colour.

Decorated Eggs

It is the custom in many places to decorate eggs in the Spring. Eggs remind people of the new life that appears in the Spring. To make a decorated chicken egg to keep, you must first blow it as described. Rinse the inside with water, then decorate the egg using paints or pens. Make stencil shapes with sticky tape to colour around, then peel them off.

▶ Blowing an egg can be difficult. Make a hole with a pin in each end of a chicken egg. Blow into one hole to force the contents into a bowl.

Pin holes at either end

After a bird has built its nest, the eggs are laid. These are incubated (kept warm), usually by the parents, until the young birds hatch out.

People used to collect the eggs of wild birds for food, or sometimes just because they looked pretty. This is no longer permitted. Some birds have become very rare because no young birds have been left to hatch out. If you know where a bird is nesting, don't draw attention to it, and don't disturb the nest.

Glazed Flowers

WARNING! some plants are poisonous — always check with an adult before you eat any flowers or leaves.

Many plants make flowers in the Spring. They are often brightly coloured to attract the insects which will pollinate them. Once pollination has taken place, seeds can start to form, and these will grow into next year's plants. This is why it is important not to pick wild flowers, because if a plant loses its flower it will also lose its seeds for the following year. Ask if you can have a few petals from garden flowers to make these glazed flowers. If you use garden primroses or roses you can eat them afterwards—but remember that some flowers are poisonous.

Separate an egg white from the yolk. Beat the white with a fork, adding a little water until the liquid is just thin enough to use as a paint. Use a new, soft paintbrush to coat the petals with the egg white. Dip the petals in castor or icing sugar and leave them to dry.

Summer

At this time of the year a lot of sunlight energy is available, so plants complete their growth. Plants and animals that need damp conditions may find it difficult to avoid drying out. Animals that are out during the day may have problems staying cool. Those that normally rely on the protective cover of darkness to feed often have to show themselves at dawn and dusk.

▲ In a drought the ground can become so dry that it shrinks, and cracks appear. The experiment on the opposite page shows you how to measure the depth of these cracks.

Heating up

On a sunny day use your hand to compare the temperature of grass with that of black tarmac. Dark and dull objects absorb a lot of heat energy and so become hotter than light and shiny objects, which reflect most of the energy back. You can use this fact to make your own solar heater. Fill a plastic bottle with

Grass

Tarmac

water and check the temperature of the water. Put the bottle in a black plastic bag and leave it in the sun. Check the temperature of the water again after a few hours. Some people use the free energy from the sun to heat the water in their house by this method. It has an extra advantage—it does not cause pollution.

Water heats up much more slowly than most

Sand   Water

materials. Test this by placing a tray of water next to a tray of sand in the sun. Check at intervals to see which feels warmer. The fact that the temperature of water does not change quickly is useful for underwater animals like fish. Before the water can become too hot for them during the day, the sun goes down and the water starts to cool again.

Hours of Sunshine

In the section on Spring weather you can make a bar chart to show the length of the day. However, even though the time between dawn and dusk might be 16 hours, the sun might actually shine for only six of those hours. You could count the hours of sunshine with a stopwatch, but here is an easier way.

Make a chart, with two columns. Down the left-hand column mark the following times: 7·00, 8·30, 10·00, 11·30, 13·00, 14·30, 16·00, 17·30, 19·00, 20·30. During one day record whether the sun was shining (√) or not shining (×) at each of these times. To find out how sunny the day was, add up the number of ticks, and multiply by ten. For example, if you have four ticks, the day was approximately 40% sunny. For animals such as butterflies, the amount of sunshine in a day is more important than the length of the day.

The Dry Season

Although there may be a lot of rain in the Summer, most of the moisture quickly evaporates into the air. As a result, the ground can become so dry that it starts to crack. If you find a drought crack, tie a heavy weight onto a piece of string and lower it into the crack. Mark the string when the weight reaches the bottom and measure the length. Check each day to see if the crack gets deeper.

Summer Storms

Summer is a time of sudden storms. Huge movements of air are caused when some areas of ground heat up more quickly than others. Large, towering clouds form, and sparks of electricity flash across the sky. A lot of rain may fall in a short time. Mammals can often sense a thunderstorm long before it is heard or seen. They become restless, and their fur stands on end.

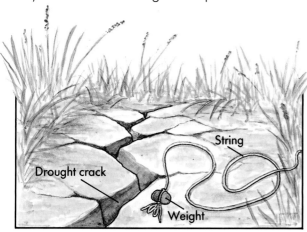

Drought crack

String

Weight

Sweaty Grass!

Plants use energy from the sun to make food in their green leaves. To do this they need to absorb water from the soil into their roots. Surplus water is **transpired** (breathed out) from the leaves. On a sunny day, place a plastic sheet on a lawn. Look under it at hourly intervals to see how much transpired water has collected on the sheet. To find out where grass gets water from when there is no rain, put the sheet out again, but overnight. On clear nights dew forms on the ground, and this provides a little extra water for plants.

Leaves in the Summer

The fact that leaves transpire so much water can cause problems for plants during a drought. However, some plants are well suited to living in dry places. Cacti lose very little water through transpiration, and can survive for years with hardly any water.

Trees are so large they transpire more water than most other plants, sometimes many litres in a day. You can observe how water moves through a leaf in the following way. Pick a leafy deciduous twig and place it in a small amount of water mixed with red cochineal dye.

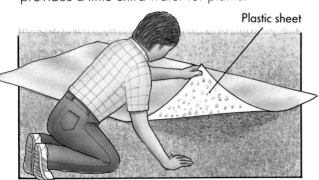

Plastic sheet

Cacti

Coping with Drought

Often, gardeners only water their plants every few days to encourage the plants to send down deeper roots looking for water. Try this experiment to see if this works. In one plastic tub put a thin layer of cotton wool. Fill a second tub with loose layers of cotton wool. Add cress seeds to both and water until they have germinated. Then keep the seeds in the first tub damp, but put water into the bottom of the second tub only when the cotton wool is nearly dry. After a week check to see what has happened to the roots.

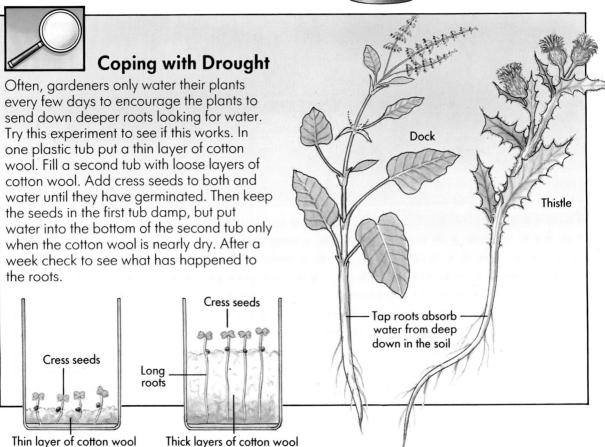

Dock

Thistle

Tap roots absorb water from deep down in the soil

Cress seeds

Cress seeds

Long roots

Thin layer of cotton wool

Thick layers of cotton wool

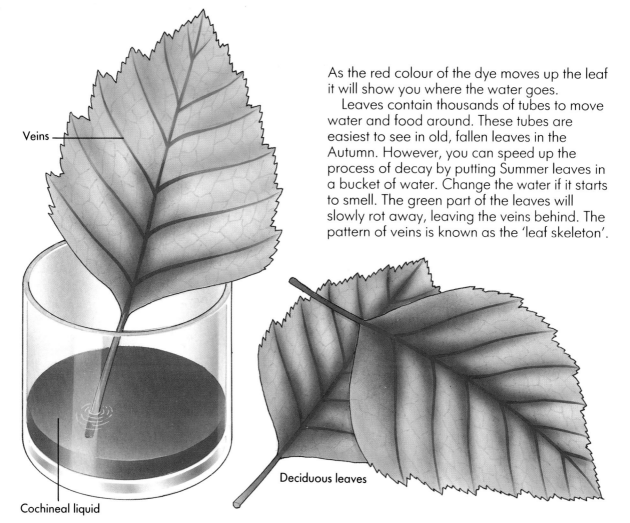

Veins

Cochineal liquid

As the red colour of the dye moves up the leaf it will show you where the water goes.

Leaves contain thousands of tubes to move water and food around. These tubes are easiest to see in old, fallen leaves in the Autumn. However, you can speed up the process of decay by putting Summer leaves in a bucket of water. Change the water if it starts to smell. The green part of the leaves will slowly rot away, leaving the veins behind. The pattern of veins is known as the 'leaf skeleton'.

Deciduous leaves

▶ The leaves of this oak tree are making sugars quickly, using the sunlight of the long days. The oak tree is now transpiring hundreds of litres of water a day. This must be replaced by absorbing water from the soil through the roots. If there is drought the tree may have to lose its leaves early to save water. The tree now has flowers. Some of these flowers will be pollinated and developed into seeds.

Animals in the Summer

In the early Summer many animals give birth to eggs or young. Often the young must be fed and guarded, and the adults are kept busy day and night. Some animals are active only during the day; these are known as **diurnal** animals. If the temperature becomes too high during the day, this can cause problems. Warm-blooded creatures must keep a constant temperature and can become too hot. Mammals lose heat by sweating or panting. As water evaporates from the skin or tongue, the body cools down.

Life by Day

Many insects are diurnal. Butterflies and dragonflies need energy from the heat of the sun to be able to fly. Most flowers, therefore, open in the day to attract diurnal insects to pollinate them.
Amphibians, such as frogs and newts, shelter in sunny weather to stop themselves drying out. Reptiles, such as snakes and lizards, sun themselves to raise their body temperature and make themselves more active.

Buddleia

Kestrel

Cranefly

Caterpillars

Dog

Thrush   Daisies   Dragonfly   Rabbit

Butterflies

Hidden Nightlife

Many animals are active only at night. They are known as **nocturnal** animals. You can reveal some of this night-time activity by making a pitfall trap.

Dig a hole in the ground and place an old jar in it, so that the top is level with the soil. Cover the jar with a piece of wood raised on four stones to keep any rain out. Put some damp soil, leaves and bark in the jar. In the morning check the trap to see what creatures have wandered past in the night and fallen in. Remember to set them free afterwards!

Life by Night

Many creatures use the cover of darkness to move around more safely. Moths drink nectar from flowers that open specially at night to attract them. Small mammals, such as mice and voles, are active too. However, life at night is not completely safe. Predators make use of the cover of darkness. Bats use 'echo location' (*see page 159*) to find insects. Owls have excellent sight and hearing. Foxes use their fine sense of smell to track down small animals.

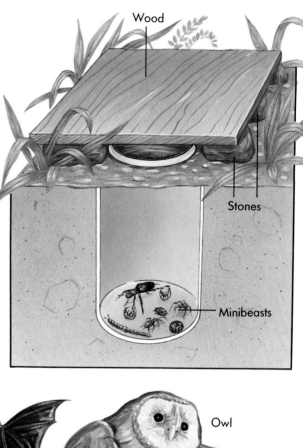

Wood

Stones

Minibeasts

Bat

Owl

Moth

Fox

Night-scented stock

Daisies close up at night

Stoats hunt day and night

Rabbits graze during the day and night

Lavender Baskets

In Summer most plants produce flowers which attract insects. When an insect visits a flower, pollination can occur and next year's seeds will start to form. Insects are attracted to flowers by their bright colours and sweet scents. You can capture the smell of lavender by making a 'Lavender Basket'.

Collect 11 lavender flowers, with 30 centimetres of stem still attached. Cut a metre length of one-centimetre-wide ribbon. Secure the base of the flower heads (1). Bend the stems back over the flower heads so that the flowers are enclosed within the stems (2). Weave the ribbon inside one stem, then outside the next, and so on around the length of the stems. Finish off with a bow in the ribbon (3).

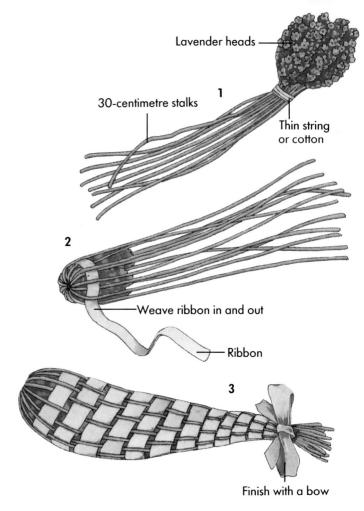

Lavender heads

30-centimetre stalks

1

Thin string or cotton

2

Weave ribbon in and out

Ribbon

3

Finish with a bow

After Flowers

The reason why plants make flowers often only becomes clear in the Autumn. Monitor a flower to see what happens—a rose would be a good choice. Gently tie a bright piece of cotton around the stem of the flower. Examine the flower every few days to see what happens after the petals fall off. Look to see where the seeds are starting to develop.

Mint Tea

Strong-smelling plants are sometimes used as foods or medicines. Try this refreshing Summer drink, using a common Summer plant. Wash a bunch of mint leaves and put them in a tea pot. Add some green tea for a stronger brew. Add hot water and leave the tea to infuse for a few minutes before pouring.

Mint leaves

Make a Flapping Butterfly

Trace the three pieces shown here onto card, making two copies of the wing. Decorate the wing, then cut the four pieces out. Hinge the wings to the body using sticky tape at A and B. Make two holes in each wing and use these to hang the wings from the holes C and D in the strip of card, using thin string. Attach a straw to the body at E from underneath. This can be pushed gently to make the wings flap. Hang the strip of card up by string using holes C and D again. By taping heavy coins to the wings you should be able to make the butterfly flap more slowly, and for longer, when you let go.

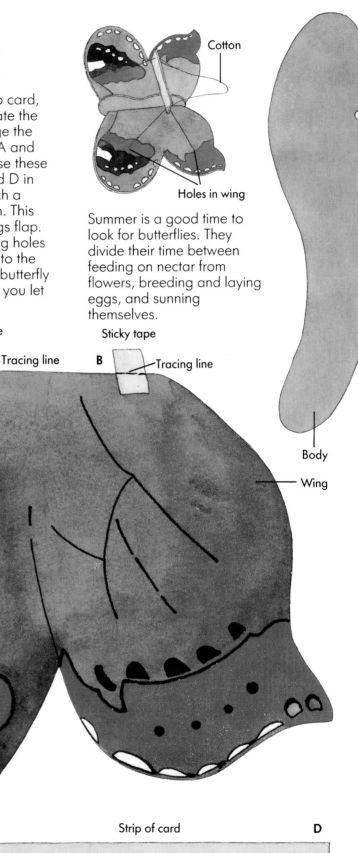

Cotton

Holes in wing

Summer is a good time to look for butterflies. They divide their time between feeding on nectar from flowers, breeding and laying eggs, and sunning themselves.

E

Body

Wing

Sticky tape

A

Tracing line

Sticky tape

B

Tracing line

C

Strip of card

D

Autumn

As Autumn draws in the days become shorter, and there is less energy from the sun for plants and animals to use. The nights may be cold and frosty, and dew often forms overnight. Plants and animals prepare for the Winter. Many will die. However, during the Autumn dead things are recycled into the soil, so the nutrients can be used again next year.

Condensing Water

If a cold night follows a warm Autumn day, **condensation** will occur. To see condensation for yourself, put a glass jar in a fridge for 30 minutes, then remove it to a warm place. The water that condenses on the glass was present in the warm air all along—but it was invisible until the air cooled.

Condensation

Star Gazing

The night sky is often very clear in Autumn. If you have binoculars, look at the Moon to see the craters. (You must never look at the Sun through binoculars—it will blind you.) Many newspapers have maps every month to help you to identify the star groupings, or constellations. Because the Earth is spinning around, the stars appear to move slowly across the sky. Only the Pole Star appears to stay in the same place in the sky, because it is positioned directly above the North Pole. When birds are migrating between countries they use the Pole Star to find their direction. Sailors, too, use stars to navigate across the oceans. People used to think that swallows migrated to the Moon—384,400 kilometres away! In fact, the record for migration goes to the Arctic Tern which can travel right around the Earth each year—a distance of about 40,000 kilometres.

Games in Fog and Dew

When warm air outside condenses overnight on the ground, a morning **dew** is the result. If the dew freezes then it is called **frost**. Sometimes water condenses in the air itself, causing **fog** or **mist**.

Fog is a great challenge to birds, especially if they are migrating. Next time it is foggy play this game in a park or playground to find out why. Ask a friend to stand still. Walk away from them until they are well out of sight. Now try to find them again by walking in a straight line. Try again, but this time call at intervals. Ask your friend to echo your call. This is how bats find prey to eat in the dark. They make a high-pitched noise which bounces back off insects, helping the bat to home in on its prey. This is called '**echo location**'.

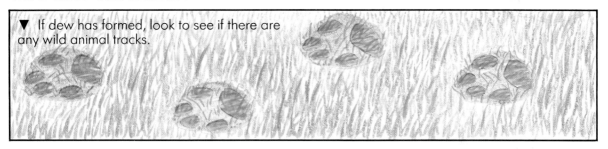

▼ If dew has formed, look to see if there are any wild animal tracks.

What is Soil?

During the Summer, plants take in the goodness, or **nutrients**, from the soil as they grow. If this continued happening throughout the year, the soil would lose all its nutrients and nothing would be able to grow in it. On the next page you can find out how nutrients are returned to the soil. If you do the experiment here you can discover what soil is made up of. Half fill a jar with soil and top it up with water. Screw the lid on tightly, shake the jar well and leave the contents to settle. The humus on top is the dead matter which provides nutrients in the soil. Sand and clay provide structure to the soil. Stones help the water to drain away, so that the soil does not become waterlogged.

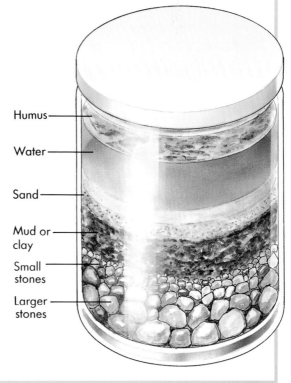

Humus

Water

Sand

Mud or clay

Small stones

Larger stones

▶ In the Autumn, deciduous trees lose their leaves. Many other plants die back. Some animals die as the weather gets colder and food becomes short. What happens to all these dead things? Fortunately there are plants and animals which feed on decaying matter. Animals which do this are called **scavengers**. Plants which live off dead matter include the **fungi**. These do not make their own food like many plants. Instead fungi absorb nutrients from dead things through their roots. You can grow fungi by keeping stale bread wet. The mould which appears is a type of fungus. Some fungi, such as mushrooms, can be eaten. However, some are extremely poisonous. The fungus in the picture is feeding off dead wood.

The Natural Way to Throw Away

In a garden or field nutrients are removed from the ground each time vegetables or flowers are picked. You can help to return nutrients to the soil by making a compost heap. Dead leaves, vegetable peelings, rotten fruit and grass cuttings can all be turned into compost. The 'rotters', such as fungi, and scavenger animals, such as worms, will feed on the dead matter breaking it down. When the decay is complete, the compost can be dug into the garden soil to replace the lost nutrients.

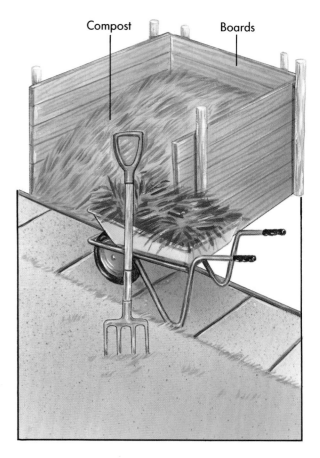

Compost   Boards

Falling Leaves

You can monitor how deciduous trees lose their leaves by choosing a particular branch on a deciduous tree. Mark 20 leaves with bright paint. Every few days record how many of the marked leaves have fallen off. Try marking leaves on different types of deciduous trees to find out which type loses its leaves first. Look for leaf scars on a twig. This is where the leaves were attached to the twig, and is the point where the water supply to the leaf was cut off, causing the leaf to die.

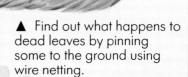

▲ Find out what happens to dead leaves by pinning some to the ground using wire netting.

Mark leaves with paint

Leaf scar

▶ Deciduous trees, such as this oak tree, often look very colourful in the Autumn. Photosynthesis in the leaves stops, and the green chlorophyl which captured the energy of the sun breaks down. The tree is covered with acorns, which are seeds. Many of these will be eaten by birds or mammals, but a few may germinate. In a hundred years they may grow into a new oak tree like the one here.

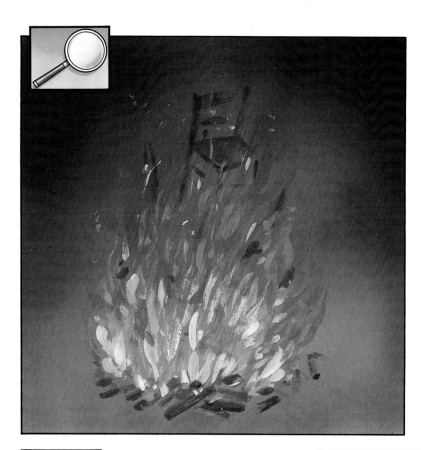

Autumn Preparations

At this time of the year animals start to prepare for the hard Winter months. Food will be difficult to find, so many animals store food to eat later in the Winter. Most mammals grow a thicker Winter coat. It is a traditional time for humans to have a bonfire, but if possible it is better that leaves and other dead plants are made into compost. If you do have a bonfire remember to check it for any hibernating animals before setting light to it.

Closing Down for the Winter

In preparation for Winter, many animals eat lots of food and then find a place to hibernate, often under the soil. Many winged insects will die because in cold weather they cannot fly well enough to find food. However, there will be insect eggs, larvae and pupae ready to hatch into new adult insects when the Spring comes. Animals that eat insects will have to change their feeding habits or lifestyles in the Winter, or they will starve. Some birds change their diet and eat seeds instead. Others migrate to countries where insects are still available.

Bats hibernate in a roost where they lower their body temperature to save energy. They must not be disturbed or they will lose vital energy which they then cannot replace. Snails seal over the entrance to their shell. It is not harmful to bring these into the warm to wake up. Give them some fresh leaves to eat before putting them back where you found them.

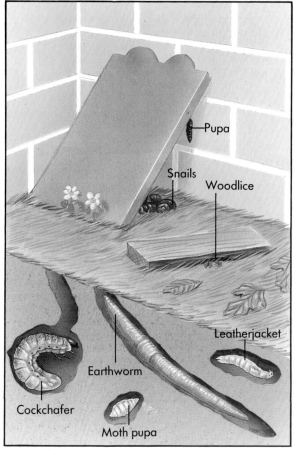

Pupa

Snails

Woodlice

Leatherjacket

Earthworm

Cockchafer

Moth pupa

Stocking Up for the Winter

Many plants produce seeds at this time of year. Often these are in the form of berries and nuts which animals will eat and collect, and so spread around. Hide some nuts in different places outside and see if you can find them the next day, and then next week. Flocks of birds strip fruit bushes bare. Some mammals form a thick layer of fat under their skin. This will be used later to provide energy, and will help to insulate the animal from the cold. In very cold weather, many warm-blooded creatures will die. They will not be able to find enough food to provide energy to stay warm.

Elderberry

Blackberry

Jay

Holly berry

Fox

Chestnut

Fir cone

Acorn

Humans Stocking Up

Equipment: ½ kilogramme apples, ½ kilogramme blackberries, 1 kilogramme sugar, lemon, water.

People lay down fat in the Winter too! They also store food. Autumn fruit can be preserved as jam. Try making this blackberry and apple jam with an adult. Wash and chop ½ kilogramme of apples, including the peel and core. Add ¼ litre of water and simmer to a pulp. Cool the pulp and squeeze it through muslin. Add ½ kilogramme of blackberries and the juice of one lemon, together with one kilogramme of sugar. Heat the mixture gently, stirring until the sugar has dissolved. Then boil until it is thick. Take great care because the jam becomes very hot. To check it is ready, put a little on a cold saucer—a skin should form. Pour the jam into warmed pots, and cover with wax discs. Seal tightly with a lid, or cellophane and an elastic band. All sorts of fruits can be used to make jam.

▶ The Earth is tilted slightly in relation to the Sun. During the Summer months, the northern hemisphere (half) of the Earth is facing the sun more directly. As a result more sunlight energy reaches the surface of the Earth. At the same time the southern hemisphere is tilted away from the sun and so has Winter. Six months later the situation is reversed. While the northern hemisphere has Winter, it is Summer in the southern hemisphere.

Plants and animals have ways of living to cope with the changing seasons, as you have seen in this book. They have often developed over time to follow the seasonal pattern of one particular area. Many people are concerned that if the weather patterns of the Earth change rapidly due to human activity some plants and animals will not be able to adapt and survive in the new conditions.

Waste not, Want not

Autumn is the time when dead things are recycled into the soil. If this recycling stopped, dead leaves would soon swamp everything and the soil would lose its goodness. Unfortunately, people do not recycle things in the same way. Trees are cut down to make paper which is then thrown into rubbish tips. Waste vegetable matter is thrown away instead of being turned into compost and returned to the soil. Glass is made from sand and then dumped. Metal ore is dug up and made into cans which are discarded. At the same time, energy is wasted and pollution caused. Find out how much of your rubbish could be recycled and then follow the example of Nature!

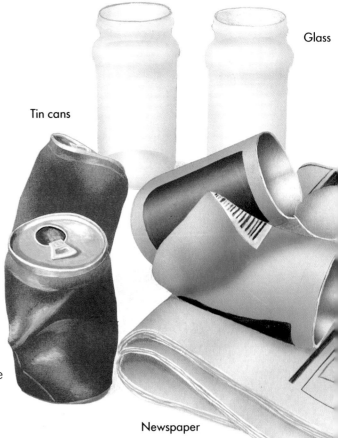

Glass

Tin cans

Newspaper

Thistle Mice

Equipment: a thistle head (or other prickly seed head), a fir cone, large black seeds (for example, poppy seeds), string, glue.

Some of the seeds made by plants in the Autumn make attractive decorations. However, don't take too many because animals need them for food to stay alive.

To make these thistle mice, break off the scales from the fir cone and dip the ends in glue. Stick these into the thistle head to make ears and feet. Make eyes and a nose by pressing in the seeds. Use a length of string to make the tail.

The seeds used here are all scattered in different ways. Thistle heads have tiny hooks which cling on to mammals' fur. Poppy seeds are contained in a 'pepper pot' head which shakes out the seeds. Fir cones open on fine days, and then the seeds hidden by its scales are blown away.

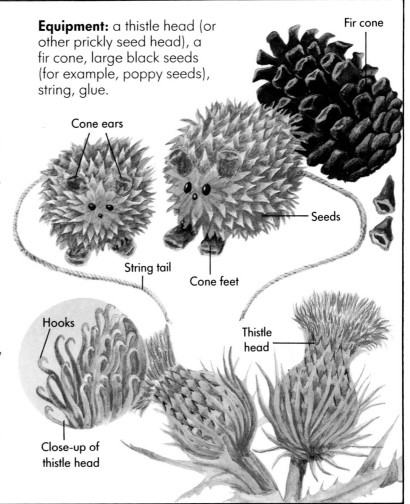

Fir cone

Cone ears

Seeds

String tail

Cone feet

Hooks

Thistle head

Close-up of thistle head

The Cycle Continues

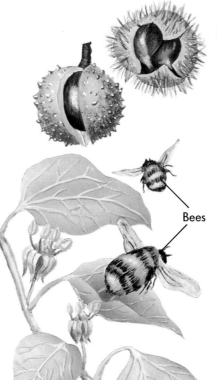

Bees

People often think that Autumn is the end of the year. Many birds leave for warmer countries. Some animals prepare to hibernate. Most insects die. Deciduous trees shed their leaves. Many plants make seeds and then die back. However, there is no beginning or end to the cycle of the seasons. Autumn is also the time when ivy comes into flower, providing food for remaining insects. The fruits and seeds everywhere will grow into plants next year. It is the rutting time for deer—the young will be born in the Spring. Take an Autumn amble and look for signs that the seasonal cycle is continuing.

Surviving the Seasons

Choose an animal or plant, and see if you can last a whole year as you battle to survive the seasons. Up to six people can play. Cut out rectangles of card, two centimetres by one centimetre to make a counter for each player. Write (or draw) or each counter one of these: **Oak, Poppy Seed, Thrush, Swallow, Dragonfly Nymph Badger.** On the reverse of the poppy seed counter write **Poppy Flower**. You will be instructed when to turn the counter over to show when the seed has grown and flowered; and when to turn it back again to show when the flower has made seeds. O the reverse of the dragonfly nymph counte write **Dragonfly Adult.** You will be instructe when the dragonfly changes from one stag

WINTER

AUTUMN

Mild days, frosty nights

Dragonfly nymphs, and **poppy seeds** are well suited to surviving the winter.
Dragonfly adults and **poppy flowers**: DIE.
Swallows: any left will STARVE.

Harsh frost

Poppy flower, dragonfly adult and **swallow**: DIE.
Badger and **thrush**: *back 1 space.*
Swallow: STARVES

Snow thaws

A square to rest on before the seasonal cycle continues.

Deep snow
Food covered up.

Thrush, dragonfly (adult only), **poppy** (flower only): DIE.
Swallow: all swallows should have migrated. Any left will STARVE.

Hedge cut
Hedges provide food for animal life.

Oak: new growth cut back. *Move back 2 spaces.*
Thrush: STARVE because no berries to eat.
Badger: food shortage. *Move back 2 spaces.*

Humans provide food

Thrush and **badger**: *move on 3 spaces.*

Early frost
Plants and insects affected.

Poppy, dragonfly (adult only): KILLED.
Swallow: migrate to Africa for Winter. *Leave the game for 3 turns until Spring arrives then rejoin at the start point.*

Sunshine and showers
Good growing conditions.

Poppy: if at flower stage, makes seed. *Turn counter over.*
Dragonfly: adult lays egg to make nymphs. *Turn counter over.*

Drought
If water is short, wil suffers.

Thrush and **swallov** move back 1 spa
Oak: *back 1 space on first round. Yo trees need water*
Dragonfly nymph: DIES when the p dries out.

166

Start point

Fine Spring weather

Nature Reserve
All wildlife is protected here.

Move your counter on 2 spaces.

Shooters and trappers
Animal life at risk.

Thrush SHOT
Swallow SHOT
Badger TRAPPED

Warm sunny weather
Plants and animals can grow quickly.

Poppy seed can grow into flower. *Turn the counter over.*
Dragonfly nymph hatches into adult dragonfly. *Turn the counter over.*

SPRING

of its life cycle to another.

All pieces start at the beginning of Spring. Put three coins in a jar. Take turns to shake out the coins. For each coin that turns up 'heads', move one square. For example if you score two heads and one tail, you move two squares. If you score three tails you stay where you are! Read the square to see if there is an instruction for your piece. If you have to move forward or back, remember to read the instructions on the new square you come to as well. If the instruction is in CAPITAL LETTERS your animal or plant has been killed. Start again, with a new piece if you like. See which piece is the first to complete a whole year, and which one goes around the most times.

Late frost
Insects and plants may die.

Swallow: no insects to feed on, so you STARVE.
Poppy: if you are at the flower stage you are KILLED. *or*: if you are a seed you survive.
Badger: delay breeding. *Move back 1 space.*

Continuous wet weather
This affects animal life.

Thrush: DIE of cold if this is your first circuit of the board. Most birds die in their first year.
Dragonfly: DIE if adult. Dragonfly nymph survives.

SUMMER

Warm showery weather

..py: seed grows into ..ower. *Turn counter ..ver. or*: flower ..akes seed. *Turn ..unter over.*
..gonfly: nymph ..atches into adult. ..rn counter over. or: ..dult lays egg. *Turn ..unter over.*

Poison sprayed on gardens and fields

Thrush, swallow and **badger** become ill. *Move back 1 space and miss a turn in the wildlife area.*
Oak: POISONED if on first circuit. Young trees are easily killed.
Dragonfly (adult or nymph): POISONED.

Wildlife area made at school
Wildlife can flourish.

All counters move on 2 spaces.

Seasons Quiz

1. We have seasons because the earth is tilted in relation to the sun.

True or False?

2. Which of these would come out at night?

True or False?

3. Which of these weather conditions is a direct result of condensation? **1.** Dew **2.** Drought **3.** Wind **4.** Clouds

True or False?

4. Which of the above returns more nutrients to the soil?

5. In the spring which of the above uses scent to mark its territory?

True or False?

Answers

1. True. During the Winter in the Northern hemisphere the North Pole is tilted away from the Sun and the northern end of the planet receives less sunlight.

2. The owl comes out at night to hunt. The hawk can only see well in the daylight.

3. Dew is caused by condensation of water vapour from the warm air onto the cold grass. Clouds are made by water vapour condensing in cold air.

4. The compost heap helps all the matter in it to break down and so returns more nutrients to the soil.

5. The fox marks its territory with a powerful scent to tell other foxes to keep out.

Glossary

Antennae The "feelers" on an insect, chiefly used to detect smell.

Cambium The part of a tree trunk where new wood cells are made.

Camouflage The use of colour and shape in order to merge into the background to avoid detection.

Carbon Dioxide The gas in the air which is breathed out by animals and taken in by plants.

Carnivore An animal which has a diet of meat (other animals).

Chlorophyll The green chemical in plants, needed to convert carbon dioxide and water into sugars.

Condensation This occurs when the invisible water present in all air becomes visible as water droplets, often as a result of a drop in temperature.

Conifer A tree in which the seeds are contained in cones.

Cycle A cycle in nature is a process which goes round in a circle and ends where it started. For example, a seed grows into a flowering plant which makes seeds again.

Deciduous Any tree which loses its leaves in the Winter.

Decomposition The rotting down of dead matter.

Dependence The way in which a particular plant or animal relies on other plants or animals for its survival.

Diurnal Creatures which are active during the day.

Dormant When a living thing is completely inactive, as in a seed which has yet to germinate, or an animal which is hibernating.

Ecology The way that living things relate to each other and their surroundings.

Ecosystem The way in which all the plants and animals in a particular area relate to each other.

Endoskeleton A skeleton inside the body—for example the bones in a human.

Evergreen A tree which has leaves throughout the year.

Exoskeleton A skeleton surrounding the body, for example as in insects.

Fungi A group of plants which do not contain chlorophyll, and so cannot make their own food.

Germination When a seed sprouts and starts to grow.

Gravity The force drawing objects towards the centre of the Earth.

Habitat The natural surroundings of a plant or animal.

Herbivore An animal which has a diet of plants.

Hibernation The state of

'shut-down' that occurs in some animals during the Winter.

Insect Any creature which has 6 legs and 3 parts to the body in the adult state.

Larva The infant stage of the insect lifecycle, before wings are formed.

Metamorphosis This describes the change in form when a larva turns into an adult.

Migration A large movement of animals, often from one country to another.

Nocturnal A creature that is active during the night.

Nutrient An essential component of soil or food, required by a plant or animal to grow.

Nymph A stage in the lifecycle of some insects, similar to a larva, although the developing wings are present.

Omnivore An animal which eats both plants and other animals.

Oxygen A gas in the air, released by green plants, and breathed in by animals.

Parasite An animal or plant which obtains its nutrients from another living plant or animal, sometimes causing it harm.

Photosynthesis The conversion of carbon dioxide and water into sugars within a green plant.

Predator An animal which

kills other animals for food.

Prey An animal which is killed by a carnivore for food.

Recycle The process of breaking materials down so they can be used again.

Reproduction The production of seeds by plants, and young by animals, in order to ensure that a species continues.

Scavenger An animal that feeds on dead and decaying matter, rather than eating live plants or killing animals.

Territory The area defended by one animal against other animals of the same species.

Transpiration The loss of water to the air through leaves.

Index

Page numbers in *italics* refer to the page where a word is first defined.

A
Acid rain *122*, 127
Acorns 12, 17, 110, 119
Algae 23, 119
Amphibians 154
Animals 36, 39, 42, 43
Antennae 53, 62
Ants 56, 73, 80–1
Arctic tern 158
Avocados 17

B
Bark 94, 95, 98, 99, 119
Bats 43, 45, 159, 162
Beaufort scale 133
Bees 18, 19, 56, 73, 78–9, 95, 114
Beetles 57, 73, 87
Berries 163
Birds 16, 41, 43, 44, 46, 47, 95, 96, 101, 112, 118, 119, 121, 125, 133, 138, 139, 141, 146, 147, 149, 154, 158, 159, 162, 163, 165
Bluebells 144
Branch scars 98
Buddleia 59
Buds 94, 100–1, 124, 144, 145
Bulbs 144
Buttercups 19
Butterflies 18, 56, 58–9, 62, 85, 151, 154, 157

C
Cabbage plants 59
Cacti 42, 152
Caddis flies 71
Cambrium layer 98, 99
Camels 42
Camouflage 71, 72
Carbon dioxide 29, 30–31, 95, 105, 126
Carnivores 40, 68
Caterpillars 58, 59, 62, 71, 72
Catkins 110, 112, 115
Centipedes 73

Chlorophyll *25*, 30, 108
Christmas rose 136
Cocoons 82
Colours 143, 156
  of insects 74
Compost 160
Condensation 29, 158
Cones 142, 165
Conifers 107, 110, *112*
Coppicing 124
Cowslip 59
Crickets 72
Crossbills 112
Crustaceans 38
Cycles, natural 17, 28, 29

D
Daisies 19
Daphnia 64
Deciduous trees *106*, 107, 137, 144, 153, 160, 161, 165
Decomposition *109*, 118, 120
Deer 39, 94, 119, 134, 165
Dehydration *107*
Dependence *118*
Deserts 28, 42
Dew *159*
Dispersal of seeds *16*, 112
Diurnal animals *154*
Dor (dung) beetles 87
Dormancy *111*
Dormice 33
Dragonflies 65–6
Drought 150, 152
Dyes, natural 148

E
Earth 164
Earwigs 73
Ecosystems 118, *119*
Eggs 36, 149
Endoskeletons 56
Evaporation *142*, 151
Evergreens *106*, 107, 137, 140
Exoskeletons 56

F
Fleas 56
Flies 54, 56

Flowers 18–22, 59, 62, 69, 78, 85, 95, 114, 115, 118, 120, 136, 144, 149, 156, 165
Fog *159*
Food 32–3, 40–1
Food plants 59
Forests 28
Foxes 119, 121, 146, 155, 163
Foxgloves 19, 21
Frogs 37, 67
Frost 136, 143, *159*
Fruits 110, 111, 114–5, 163, 165
Fungi 23, 119, 120, *160*

G
Germination *12–3*, 24–5, 110, 113
Gills *67*
Girdle scars *100*
Grains 22
Grasses 22, 31
Grasshoppers 72
Gravity 24, 26
Greenfly 36

H
Habitats *54*
Harlequin larvae 64
Heartwood 98
Herbivores 40, 68
Hermaphrodites 84
Hibernation 43, 134, *139*, 146, 162
Hoverflies 69, 73
Humans 36, 39, 58
Hyacinth bulbs 140

I
Ice 134, 135, 143
Insects 18, 19, 22, 38, 94, 95, 101, 118, 119, 120, 139, 155, 156, 162, 165
  colours, 74
  identifying 56–7, 62
Insulation 134, 135, 138
Ivy 119

L
Ladybirds 57, 73, 74–5

Larvae 58, 65, 71, 75, 79, 81, 87
Lavender 156
Leaf litter 118, *120*
Leaves 94, 96, 100, 101, 102–9, 145, 152–3, 160–1
Lenticels 94, 99
Lesser celandine 136, 144
Lice 55, 56, 58, 73
Lichens 23, 119
Light 24–5, 30–1
Lilac 59
Lizards 37, 44

M
Maggots 65
Mammals 138, 141, 146, 151, 154, 155, 162, 163
Marigold 59
Metamorphosis 37, 58, 65
Mice 40, 41, 134, 155
Migration 44
Millipedes 57
Mist *159*
Mistletoe 121
Money spiders 70
Mosses 121
Moths 63, 155
Mustard and cress 15

N
Nectar 18, 19, 59, 62, 69, 78
Nettles 59, 148
Nocturnal animals *155*
Nutrients *159*, 160
Nuts 110, 112, 141, 163
Nymphs, dragonfly 65

O
Oak 137, 145, 153, 161
Omnivores *40*
Ovaries *114*
Owls 40, 41, 121, 134, 139, 155
Oxygen 28, 29, 30–1, 95, 102, 105, 126

P
Papermaking 122, 123

Parasites 56, 121
Parasitic plants 31
Pheromones *63*
Phloem 98
Photosynthesis 29
Pigments *108*
Pill bugs 73
Pitfall traps 52
Plant galls 120
Pods 110, 112
Pollarding 124
Pollen *114*, 115
Pollination 18, 19, 20
Pollution 122
Ponds 23, 64–5, 67
Pooters 52
Poppies 17
Potatoes 33
Predators 68
Prey 68
Primrose 144, 149
Proboscis *18*
Pupae 58, 62, 65, 81

R
Rabbits 36, 39
Ragwort 59
Rain 142, 151
Rain forests 122, 126–7
Recycling rubbish 164
Reproduction *17–19*
Reptiles 37, 44, 154
Rock rose 59
Root hairs 98
Roots 94

S
Sap *121*
Sapwood 98
Scavengers 42, 160
Seeds 12–7, 22, 24–5, 95, 110–4
Segmented bodies 53, 57
Sexton beetles 87
Shrews 42, 43
Silver birch 137
Skeletons 56
Slugs 147, 155
Snails 36, 58, 64, 84, 139, 147, 155
Snakes 37, 44
Snow 134, 135, 140
Soil 159
Spiders 68–70
Spiracles 53
Spores 23
Squirrels 95, 99, 112, 118, 147, 163

Stamens *114*
Stars 158
Stick insects 38
Stomata *106*
Sugars 29, 30, 32, 33,
     100, 105, 108
Sun 142,150–1, 152,
     158, 164
Sunflowers 17
Sunlight 24–5, 30–1,
     100, 102, 104, 105,
     120
Swallows 44
Sweet William 59

T
Temperature 134, 143,
     150
Terminal buds *101*
Territories *147*
Thistle 152, 165
Thrushes 84, 133, 147
Thunderstorms 151
Toads 42, 67
Transpiration 28, 29,
     106, 107, 152
Traps 52–3
Trees 12, 27, 28, 136–7,
     144–5, 147, 152–3,
     160, 161, 165
  age of 93, 94
  deciduous *106*, 107
  girth of 93, 96
  height of 93, 95
Twigs 92, 94, 98, 99,
     100–1, 124

V
Vacuum trap 52
Vole 135, 139, 155
Vultures 42

W
Wasp beetles 73
Wasps 73, 79
Water 26–9, 30, 42, 98,
     100, 105, 106, 107,
     108, 134–5, *142*,
     150
Water boatmen 64
Water fleas 64
Water habitats 64–7
Water skaters 65
Weather forecasting
     133, 142

Wind 133
Wood 122–7
Woodlice 38, 55, 58, 73,
     147, 155
Worms 58, 73, 82–3

X
Xylem 98

Photographic Acknowledgements

The publishers wish to thank the following for supplying photographs for this book:

Page 12 Rosie Harlow; 17 ZEFA; 23 Rosie Harlow; 25 Nature Photographers; 28 ZEFA; 33 Rosie Harlow; 39 N.H.P.A./R. Tidman (top), ZEFA (bottom); 43 Dr. Robert Stebbings; 54 Heather Angel/Biofotos; 65 Nature Photographers; 66 Nature Photographers; 70 N.H.P.A./ N.R. Coulton; 76 Nature Photographers; 77 N.H.P.A.S. Dalton; 79 Swift Picture Library; 81 N.H.P.A./G.B. Bernard; 96 Rosie Harlow; 100 N.H.P.A./L. Campbell; 105 N.H.P.A./S. Dalton; 107 ZEFA; 110 N.H.P.A./S. Dalton; 114 N.H.P.A./S. Dalton; 115 N.H.P.A./B. Hawkes; 118 N.H.P.A./S. Dalton; 119 Heather Angel/ Biofotos; 120 Rosie Harlow; 122 Rosie Harlow; 124 N.H.P.A./E.A. Janes; 126 Nature Photographers; 127 Rosie Harlow; 135 ZEFA; 137 ZEFA; 145 ZEFA; 146 N.H.P.A./N. Dennis; 150 N.H.P.A./A. Bannister; 153 ZEFA; 160 N.H.P.A./S. Dalton; 161 ZEFA; 162 NASA.

Picture Research: Elaine Willis